Miyamoto Musashi

&

Shuriken

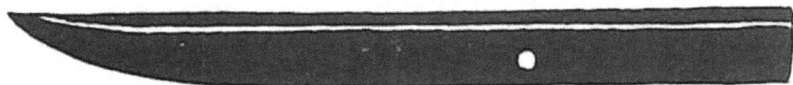

By Naruse Kanji 成瀬関次
Translation by Eric Shahan シャハン・エリック

© 2020 Eric Michael Shahan
All Rights Reserved
ISBN: 978-1-950959-29-7

Translator's Introduction:

While Shuriken, originally referred to as "throwing stars" in the West, are associated with Ninja and Ninjutsu, there doesn't seem to be any historical documentation of this. Some sources refer to Shuriken-like weapons or throwing short or long swords as a gambit when faced with multiple opponents. The earliest source on Shuriken being used is a book from the fourth year of Genwa (1618) the *Gunpojiyoshu*. The book is a collection of knowledge from the previous two centuries of war covering everything from castle layout to defense against Ninja. One interesting section is titled *On the topic of throwing Taimatsu* 投げ松明の事. A Taimatsu is a type of torch. The entry reads:

It looks much like a Taimatsu, but the size depends on the person. It is important that you are comfortable holding it. This Taimatsu is also known as Shi-ri-ken. However it is not for striking people. You throw it when fighting at night.

The word *Shi-ri-ken* is in the Hiragana alphabet しりけん, however this seems to suggest this entry is referring to Shuriken.

The Samurai Nita holding a Taimatsu in this late 19th century woodblock print by Yoshitoshi

Kanji Naruse, in his 1941 book *Shuriken*, speculates on the origins of Shuriken. He believes they developed from the concept of *Uchi Mono*, which is when a Samurai uses any weapon at hand as a projectile weapon. This refers to throwing weapons not designed as projectiles like a knife, short sword or long sword. The other major influence was *Uchine*, the Japanese throwing arrow. The Uchine is an archer's last-minute countermeasure when his bow broke. Kanji says, *If the Uchi Mono is the father, then Uchine is the mother of Shuriken. So Shuriken evolved from weapons thrown as a last resort to a fully developed weapon.*

(Below) Examples of Uchine designs reproduced by Fujita Seiko from various historical documents

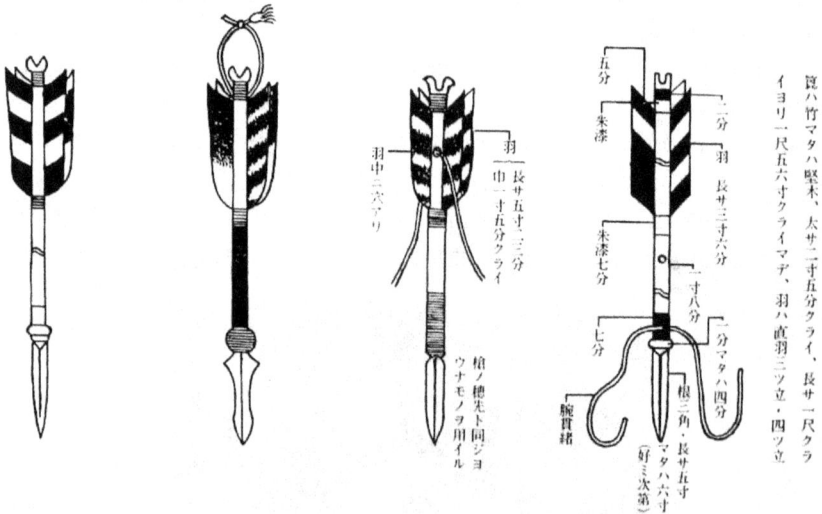

(Below) Holding and throwing techniques as illustrated by Fujita Seiko.

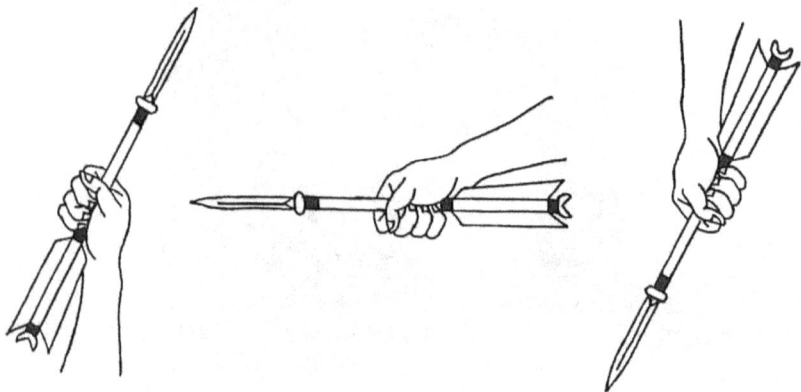

Introduction to the Contents of this Book

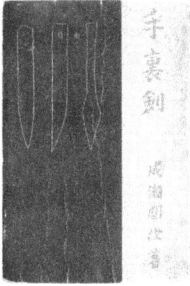

Chapters 1 & 2
Miyamoto Musashi and Shuriken
From *Shuriken* by Kanji Naruse
Published 1941

Chapter 1 is a translation of the *Miyamoto Musashi and Shuriken* section of Kanji Naruse's book *Shuriken*. Kanji Naruse was a martial arts researcher and instructor of Negishi School Shuriken. In this selection, Kanji Naruse discusses the origins of Musashi's Shuriken art using various historical documents. He also discusses Musashi's surprisingly influential connection to the famous Yagyu family and how a duel between Musashi and a member of the Yagyu family caused the Yagyu to develop new techniques to defend against an opponent throwing Shuriken.

In Chapter 2, Kanji Naruse recreates the Shuriken techniques employed by Musashi in duels.

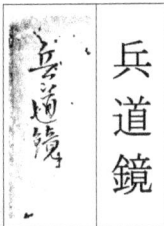

Chapter 3
Excerpt from:
The Mirror of the Martial Way
By Miyamoto Musashi. Written in 1605.

Chapter 3 is a selection from Miyamoto Musashi's own writing. He wrote about Shuriken in one of his earliest books called *The Mirror of the Martial Way*. This book has only recently been authenticated as being written by Musashi. In addition, several versions of this book exist, each with slight differences. This chapter will look at two versions of the chapter on Shuriken from *The Mirror of the Martial Way*.

Chapters 4 ~ 6
Excerpts from:
An Illustrated Guide to Shuriken
By Fujita Seiko Published 1964.

In *An Illustrated Guide to Shuriken* the author, the 14th inheritor of the Koga School of Ninjutsu Fujita Seiko, introduces documents related to Chishin Ryu, New Learning School, a Shuriken school that was founded by the descendants of Miyamoto Musashi. In addition, Fujita Seiko provides an illustrated explanation for how these Shuriken techniques are done.

Chapter 7
Excerpts from:
Heiho Kadensho written in 1631 *& Lessons on Becoming A Polished Jewel (A Great Human)* written in 1645
By Yagyu Munenori

This chapter contains translations of Yagyu School documents that mention Shuriken. The first extract is from the *Heiho Kadensho written in 1631* by Yagyu Munenori. Yagyu Munenori was a feudal lord and the official sword instructor to the Tokugawa Shogun. The second extract, also written by Yagyu Munenori is from the *Lessons on Becoming A Polished Jewel (A Great Human)* written in 1645. The section titled *Uchi Mono,* or *Striking Weapons* discusses Shuriken.

Table of Contents

Miyamoto Musashi and Shuriken

Cover of *Shuriken* 手裏剣
by Naruse Kanji 成瀬関次 1888 ~ 1948

Naruse Kanji is pictured on the right with his Oei Bizen 應永備前 Katana, which was forged in the Muromachi Era (1394-1428.)

In his famous 1941 book, Naruse Sensei devotes 2 chapters to examining the history of Miyamoto Musashi's Shuriken art. He scoured historical documents related to Musashi's life and found a wealth of information that shows the strong influence Shuriken had on Musashi's approach to marital arts and how he used them in combat. *Shuriken* is the first book to five the history of Japanese Shuriken.

Naruse Kanji was a practitioner of Negishi School Shuriken and 根岸流手裏剣術 and Kuwana Domain Yamamoto School Iai Sword Drawing 桑名藩伝山本流居合術.

宮本武藏

宮本武藏が、手裏劍術の達人であつたといふことは、吉川さんの宮本武藏には書かれてゐない。もつとも、吉川さんのは小說で、必ずしも記錄によらなければならぬといふ束縛はないのだから、あれでもよいわけであるが、今後もし日本手裏劍史を編む者があるとすれば、一方の主流をなすであらうほどに、顯著な、そして豐富な文献と事蹟とが殘つてゐるのである。

宮本武藏の傳記といふものは、十が十とも異說の交錯で、その出生地すら分明してゐない。かうした異說傳中の標準的な『略傳記』といへば、武藏の死後十年目の承應三年に、かれの養子で、當時豐前國小倉の城主小笠原右近太夫忠眞の家老職となつてゐた宮本伊織が立石した、『小倉の碑文』がそれであらう。多少の修飾は免れないとしても、その筆者は、肥後國熊本細川侯の菩提寺たる泰勝寺の住持春山和尙

手裏劍

10

Miyamoto Musashi and Shuriken

The fact that Miyamoto Musashi was an expert at Shuriken Jutsu, the art of throwing hand spikes, does not appear anywhere in Yoshikawa Eiji's historical novel *Miyamoto Musashi*. Since the book Mr. Yoshikawa wrote is a work of fiction, he does not have to strictly abide by the information contained in historical records. However, if anyone was looking to write a history of Shuriken Jutsu in Japan, they would find that Miyamoto Musashi represents the start of a major Shuriken lineage and that there is a bounty of remarkable historic documents to research.

The records and physical evidence pertaining to Miyamoto Musashi is convoluted and contradictory. If you were to read ten sources, you would end up with ten different versions of the story. Even such simple facts such as the location of his birth are unclear. Amongst all the many texts with their varying accounts the one known as Ryaku Denki, the *Abbreviated Record* is considered to be the standard. The *Abbreviated Record* is carved into the Musashi Kokura Monument. It was erected in 1654, on the initiative of Musashi's adoptive son, Miyamoto Iori.

At the time, Miyamoto Iori was serving as elder adviser to the lord of Kokura Castle Ogasawara Ukin Dayu Tadazane (1596～1667) in Higo Domain. Though there is some idealization that invariably occurs in such projects, the author was a man named Shunzan, who was the head priest at Taishoji Temple. This is the temple that contains the family grave of Lord Hosokawa of Kumamoto, Higo Domain.

で、この人は、生前武藏と親交の深かつた上に、聞えた高德者であつたから、十分信憑するに足るものと思へる。

更に、この碑文が、小笠原忠實の內命も手傳つて出來たといふ一事と、それから文中に強調された若干の語句とか、ともに手裏劍術に關係のあることを見逃してはならない。全文は漢語で書かれてゐるが、その箇所だけを書きぬいて見ると、

或飛二眞劍一、或投二木戟一、北者走者、不レ能三逃避一、其勢恰如レ發三强弩一百發百中養由無レ蹂二于斯一也。（或ひは眞劍を飛ばし、或ひは木戟（木劍のこと）を投げ、逃ぐる者走る者、逃避するに術がない。その勢、恰も强力な石弓を發するが如く、百發百中で、養由の妙術も、これ以上とは思はれない。）

といふ意味になる。文中養由の二字が何のことだか一向解き難いなどゝ云つてゐる者もあるが、これは支那の傳說的武勇傳中の人物の名で、弓を射または矢を投げその技神に入り、一たびかれの狙ひを受けた最後、嘗て逃れ得た者がなかつたといはれた弓聖養由基を指したものである。最も古い記錄としては、『春秋左氏傳』

The priest Shunzan was a friend and confidant of Musashi while the great swordsman was still alive. Since this priest was a man of unimpeachable moral virtue, we can confidently say his account meets our standards of trustworthiness.

In addition, this inscription contains details that came directly from Lord Ogasawara Tadazane. Most importantly there are a few small sections that refer to Shuriken Jutsu. While these references are very brief, we cannot allow even a single one to escape scrutiny.

The entire inscription is written in Kanbun, or Chinese-style with only Kanji and not using the native Japanese Hiragana or Katakana alphabets. Here is the first section that mentions Shuriken:

He also threw swords or he threw wooden spears (wooden spear-shaped knives.) Those trying to flee, run or evade found themselves without any method to respond. The power in his throwing technique was such that it is equivalent to that of an arrow fired by a crossbow. His skill recalls the famous phrase "Hyaku-hatsu Hyaku-chu" Firing a hundred shots and hitting dead-center every time. No doubt Musashi's abilities exceeded even the supernatural skill of the Chinese warrior Yoyu.

In the middle of the above passage the two Kanji name 養由 Yoyu really stands out. The name Yoyu probably has more than a few people scratching their heads. This is because he was a legendary warrior from China. Tales about Yoyu praise his skill as an archer, as well as his almost inhuman ability to throw an arrow with his hand. Realizing you were his target would be your last thought. No one could escape Yoyu's aim and he was thus known as Yoyu Ki, Saint of the Bow. The oldest record of his exploits is contained in the *Commentary of Zuo on the Spring and Autumn Annals*. The book is by Zuo Qiuming and was written in the 4th century BC.[1]

---

[1] Legends say that Yoyu was able to fire a bow with a draw weight strong enough to pierce seven suits of armor. He could also strike a dragonfly at the base of its wings. Yoyu could stand a hundred paces away from a willow tree, yet still hit the leaves 100 times out of 100 tries.

成公十六年晉楚鄢陵の戰の條に見えてゐる。日本でいつたら、鎭西八郎爲朝のやうな存在である。

さてこの養由の意味が判然すれば、全文自から明瞭となり、手裏劍の妙術者でもあつた武藏の一面が髣髴として來る。

武藏が、どうした經路でそれを會得し修鍊して來たかは不明だが、それを修鍊するに至つた動機が那邊から出たかを思はしむるに足る文献がある。

『丹治峰拘筆記』に。

　……武藏幼年より父が兵法を見こなし、常に誹謗す。無二、子たりといへども、そのことによつて心に叶はず。ある時無二、楊子を手づから削るに、武藏一間をへだて、ゐたり。無二その小刀をもつて、手裏劍に武藏をうつ。武藏おもてをそむけ、れば、小刀は後の柱にたちぬ。無二甚だ怒りて、平日我が兵法をなみするは不都合なりとて、更に手裏劍にてこれをうたむとせしに、武藏はまた面をそむけてのがれぬ。されど遂に父の怒りにふれて、家を出で播州にいたり、母方の叔父某の僧となれる庵にゆきぬ。時に九歳なり。

Yoyu took part in the Battle of Yanling in the 16th year of the Duke Cheng of Lu's reign 575 BC. In Japan his exploits recall those of Minamoto no Tametomo (1139 ~ 1170), also known as Chinzei Hachirō Tametomo. Tametomo is famous for sinking an enemy battleship with a single arrow by puncturing its hull below the waterline.

Now that the reference to Yoyu has been explained, Musashi's status as a master of the Shuriken arts becomes vividly clear. Considering how significant this facet of Musashi's life is, it is not clear how he acquired such consummate skill in throwing Shuriken. However, we can speculate as to where his motivation to train came from based on the book Tanji Hokin wrote in 1727 called *Record of Tanji Hokin.* The passage is as follows:

From a very young age Musashi learned martial arts from his father, but ridiculed his father's art. Though Musashi was just a child Muni (his father) never treated him as such. One day Muni was whittling toothpicks out of a piece of wood. He noticed Musashi on the other side of the room, about 180 centimeters away. Muni, using the small knife he had been whittling with, threw it as a Shuriken at Musashi. Musashi dodged, moving his face away, and the small knife stuck in the doorframe behind him. His father exploded with rage,

"Even though I have been training you in my martial arts every day you have completely disregarded the martial arts I have taught you! This is unacceptable!"

Muni took out another Shuriken and threw it at Musashi. This too Musashi avoided by moving his face away. However, eventually Musashi became unable to endure his father's rage and left to live with an un-named uncle on his mother's side. The man lived as a monk in a small hermitage. Musashi was nine years old at the time.[2]

---

[2] *Record of Tanji Hokin* was originally called *Record of Lord Genshin (Miyamoto Musashi) of Bushu, the Great Father of Sword Fighting* 兵法大祖武州玄信公伝来. The author was a Shihan, instructor, of Nitenichi School of Sword.

とあるのがそれである。

これで見ると、武藏の父親新免無二齋は、相當に粗暴な人であり、かつ楊枝など削る種類の小刀をもつてする手裏劍術に巧みであつたことが領け、同時に、當年僅か九歳の幼少な武藏が、それを巧にかはしたことからして、すでにそのころから手裏劍術と交渉のあつたことが、これでうかゞはれるのである。

勿論、かれは見様見まねで父親無二齋のうつ有様を模倣し、後更に自ら研究工夫した上のことゝ思はれるのであるが、その修錬に關する記録はなくて、一足飛びに、手裏劍で敵と眞劍に仕合つた場合が『二天記』『二刀流實錄』『武道寶鑑』に出てゐる。『二天記』のは、簡略ではあるが、正しい記録であるだけに信が置ける。

武藏伊賀國にて宍戸何某と云ふ者鎖鎌の上手也。野外に出で勝負を決す。宍戸鎌を振り出すを武藏短刀を抜き宍戸が胸を打貫き立所に斃れしを進て討果す。宍戸が門弟抜連れ各打て懸る。武藏直ちに大勢を追崩せば四方に逃去す。武藏悠然として引去る。

From this passage we can determine that Musashi's father Shinmen Munisai was quite a violent fellow. Moreover, using the kind of small knife you use to shave toothpicks as a Shuriken shows a phenomenal level of skill. At the same time, Musashi was only nine years old, yet despite his youth he was able to avoid a Shuriken thrown by an expert. Clearly we can see by this age Musashi had extensive training in the Shuriken throwing arts.

It goes without saying that, initially, Musashi merely mimicked the way his father Munisai modeled throwing and then later adapted and developed it into his own style. However, though this seems to be the way Musashi's Shuriken technique developed, there is no record of when or how he trained. Instead, we suddenly out of nowhere have a record of Musashi using a Shuriken to fell an opponent in a duel. This tale is recorded in:

- *Nitenki : Record of the Niten School* (published in 1778 by Toyoto Kagehide from Kumamoto Domain, where Musashi spent his final years.)
- *Nito Ryu Jitsuroku : Record of the Two-Sword School* (Unknown)
- *Budo Hokan : Treasury of Martial Arts* (Unknown)

While the Nitenki is a condensed account of Musashi's life, it nonetheless is fundamentally trustworthy. The duel involving Musashi using a Shuriken in a duel is as follows:

In Iga Domain Musashi encountered Shishido So-and-So who was a master of Kusari Gama, the chain and sickle. They arranged to have a duel in a field. Shishido brought out his chain and sickle and began to spin it. In response Musashi drew his Tanto, knife, and threw it into Shishido's chest. The knife stuck all the way in and Shishido fell over, dead. All of Shishido's disciples drew their swords and rushed at Musashi. Musashi immediately charged them, causing the disciples to flee in all directions. Musashi calmly sheathed his sword and left.

宮本武藏が、まだ青年の武者修業時代に、伊賀上野在住の野武士宍戸信州の鎖と闘ひ、手裏剣をもつてこれを殺したといふ事實で、武藏が生涯六十餘度の仕合中、京都の吉岡一黨との決闘と、後の船島で佐々木小次郎と闘つて破つたことゝの二つが、代表的な大仕合として著聞してゐるが、これはかれが若干回の仕合による經驗を積んだ後、卽ち腕に自信が出來てから後の決闘で、梅軒の鎖鎌に向つた時は、いはゆる修業時代であり、かつ思ひも寄らぬ異樣な武器──嘗て前例のない、梅軒の工夫創意になるこの始末におへぬ新武器新武術にかゝつたのだから、かれとしては、十三歳にしてはじめて新當流の有馬喜兵衞に打ち勝つた時とともに、生涯での危機であつたことゝ思はれる。

その闘ひの模様であるが、壯齡かつ熟達の宍戸梅軒は、左手に長大な陣鎌を振りかざし、その柄の末端につけた長い鎖の先の分銅を、右手でビュウビュウと振り廻しながら迫つて來る。すでに幾人かの敵を殪した經驗と、その都度に得た新工夫とは、飛道具に非ざる限り、如何なる武器武術といへども、かれの前には敵でなかつ

When Miyamoto Musashi was still young and still doing *Musha Shugyo*, travelling around Japan looking for chances to train or duel, he ended up in the Ueno area of Iga Domain. There he encountered Shishido Baiken, a Samurai turned Nobushi, or an ascetic who had devoted himself entirely to refining his martial arts. In the end, Musashi defeated Shishido's chain and sickle with a Shuriken. Of the sixty-odd duels Musashi fought, two truly stand out. One is the series of battles with members of the Yoshioka clan in Kyoto and the other is his duel with Sasaki Kojiro on Boat Island. However, these two well-known episodes are from later in Musashi's career, after he had gained experience from engaging in numerous battles when he was young. In other words, the later duels took place when he was more confident in his abilities.

Musashi was still working to develop his technique when he fought Shishido Baiken's chain and sickle technique. In that battle, Musashi found himself facing a man armed with a peculiar and unpredictable weapon, one he had never encountered before. Musashi was not only fighting against the ingenious weapon Baiken had developed, but also an unfamiliar and entirely new martial art. We can only surmise that in this duel Musashi was facing the greatest threat to his life he had encountered since his first victory at age 13 over Arima Kihei of the Shinto School.

Before I describe the encounter, I would first like to mention that Shishido Baiken was not only in the prime of his life, but also an experienced practitioner of martial arts. He was holding a Jin-gama, a large soldier's sickle, in his left hand. A long chain was attached to the handle with a Fundo, or weight, attached to the end of the chain. With his right hand he spun the chain that whirled with a *Whoosh, Whoosh* sound, as he advanced on Musashi. Baiken had already faced off against other Samurai and killed them. Further, each time he faced an opponent he developed new improvements and tricks to add to his technique. Other than thrown weapons, Baiken had faced every sort of weapon and every sort of martial art, and found them lacking.

た。

しかし、梅軒の鎖鎌の精妙を傳聞しながら、これを除けて通らなかつた武藏の意中にも、また一つの成算があつた。

「破る。破り得る。手裏劍の一手だ。」といふ確信がそれであつたのだ。

かれには幼少からの手裏劍の武術熟技があつた上、「刀も武術の内」といふ一つの信條から、適當な寸法と、投擲するに必要な釣合ひとをあらかじめ調整して置いた短刀を、常に、右手で拔くに便利のやうに、左前半又は右後半に帶してゐた。

いま梅軒の精妙な武術に卽應すべく、かれ一流の懸け引が行はれた。かれは、梅軒の意表外に出づることなく、左手に太刀を持ち、ずんとそれを延ばして切先を上に鉛直線に構へた。勿論左半身の體形で、「サァその鎖で思ふ存分この太刀を卷き落せ。」といはんばかりであつたが。右手はひそかに手裏劍に打つべき短刀の柄をしつかと握つてゐた。

後年に傳はつてゐる、その時の形の別説としては、「刀を左手にもち輕い右脇構

However, despite all this talk of Biken's prowess and sublime chain and sickle technique, the fact remains it was not sufficient to defeat Musashi. He failed to realize Musashi had a calculated plan and that he had a firm belief in one rule:

Break them. Make them give you a chance to shatter them. That is what you achieve with one throw of the Shuriken.

From a young age Musashi had undergone extensive training in the martial art known as Shuriken and one particular lesson was drilled into him,

The Katana is only one part of martial arts.

As he stood waiting with the left side of his body forward and the right side of his body angled away, he had already memorized the shape and weight of his Shuriken. Musashi had already judged the proper distance to his target and positioned the Tanto knife in his hand. This positioning is made easier by the fact Musashi was long accustomed to drawing and holding his knife with his right hand.

Now Musashi was ready to respond to Baiken's refined martial technique and Musashi employed the hallmark strategy of his school. He did not wait for Baiken to launch his surprise attack, but held his Katana in his left hand and extended it fully until the sword was in a straight line with the tip pointed directly at Baiken. Of course Musashi had adopted a stance with his left side facing forward and it seemed to beckon,

So then hurl that chain with all your might and wrap up my sword and yank it down!

All the while Musashi's right hand was firmly gripping the handle of his Tanto which he intended to throw as a Shuriken.

剣裏手

へとし、左半身、如何にも刀を鞘で岔かれまいとするかの如き用心深い態を装ひな
がらも、右手は矢張り短刀の柄を摑んだ。」としてゐるが、どつちでもよい。飽く
まで "刀で闘ふ" といふ風を見せて――たとひ右手が短刀にかかつてゐても、それ
は、逆二刀で來るとしか思へぬ態勢で相對した。

梅軒は、敵の刀なり手なりを巻きからめるといふ恰好で、分銅を打ち振り打ち振
り實は敵の眞向眉間を狙つて分銅を打ちつけ、ひるむところへ鎌をかけるといふ心
意で追つてゆく。　武藏はぢりぢりと退く。　梅軒が最後にぶるツと振つた分銅が恐ろ
しい唸りを生じて武藏の顔面に飛んだのと、武藏がヒョッと顔をそむけて分銅をか
はしながら、その右手の短刀が、梅軒の胸に飛んだのとは同時であり、武藏が辛く
も顔をかはした一刹那、殆ど右横面一寸か五分かのところを、六角形に削つた分銅
が風を切つて進んだ時に、梅軒は「オォ」と低い呻き聲を發してよろめいた。　武藏
の手裏劍に打つた短刀が、深く胸を貫いたからである。　同時に、武藏の打つた右手
がそのまゝ大刀の柄へかゝつた一瞬、殆ど目にも止まらぬ早わざで屈伸して梅軒の

A later version of this duel describes the scene differently.

He held the Katana in his left hand, standing with the left side of his body forward but with his right side turned slightly to the front. He was completely prepared for the chain to entangle his sword. His right hand, of course, was gripping the handle of his Tanto.

Though this description differs, it doesn't really matter. In the end Musashi made a great show of "I am going to fight with my Katana." While Musashi's right hand may have been gripping the handle of his Tanto, Baiken would have presumed that his opponent was utilizing some kind of Nito Ryu, two-sword style.

One of Baiken's approaches was to wrap up the hands or the sword of his opponents. He would also launch multiple strikes with the Fundo weight, spinning the chain, striking and spinning again, all the while seeking to hit his adversary straight in the face, right between the eyebrows. His ultimate intent is to attack with his sickle, just as the opponent is flinching away from the Fundo weight coming at his eyes.

In this duel, Musashi slowly edges backwards as Baiken spins his chain. As the weight swings around to the top of its arc, Baiken gives it a mighty twist and it flies at Musashi's face. Musashi whips his face aside and, as the weight sails by, he throws the Tanto he has been holding in his right hand and it flies into Baiken's chest.

In that life or death instant, Musashi narrowly avoids the hexagonal cut weight at the end of Baiken's chain. It passed 3 centimeters or maybe even 1.5 centimeters from his face. Baiken emits a low groan of *Ohh!* and staggers. The Tanto knife Musashi had thrown as a Shuriken is buried deep in Baiken's chest. At the same time, Musashi shifts his right hand, that he had just used to throw the Shuriken, to join his left hand on the handle of his Katana. Baiken's head begins to lean forward. In one rapid movement, so fast it wouldn't register to the eye, Musashi advances on the man directly across from him, and cuts him from the top of his head down to the tip of his nose.

眞向を鼻先まで割つてゐた。

かくてこの難仕合に武藏は辛くも勝つことを得た。そして、この決鬪から生れた
のが武藏の二刀流であつた。武藏は、二刀流を自ら編み出しながら、あまりそれを
用ひなかつたと色々な本に書いてあるのは、まだその本當の眞相にぶつつからぬか
らであつて、武藏は短刀を手裏剣に打つたこの逆二刀の妙用を後世に殘してゐる。
これは、せつぱ詰つた場合に用ひるかれの〝秘術〟だから、他の劍豪の傳書同様
に、本には書いてない。たゞ事實として『二天記』に殘つてをり、後世更にそれを
想察敷衍して、『二刀流實錄』『武道寶鑑』などに記されてゐるに過ぎない。

『日本劍道史』には、

……二刀流の一派に、溫故知新流といふのがある。これは、宮本武藏の二天一流から出た末流
で、俗に逆二刀流と呼ばれ、長刀を左に短刀を右に構へ、右の短刀を手裏剣に打つてすばやく
斬り込むのであると傳へられてゐるが、その傳統は絕え正しい記錄は傳はつてをらぬ。たゞ備

Thus, despite the extreme difficulty and danger of this battle Musashi emerged victorious. Further, Musashi's Nito Ryu, two-sword style, was born out of this duel. Many books about Musashi talk about how he developed his two-sword style, but then go on to talk about how he rarely employed it. This runs counter to the reality of what happed. Musashi employed his Tanto by throwing it as a Shuriken in what can only be described as a reversal of how the two-sword style is perceived. This subtle and brilliant use is what he left to later generations.

Since this was a *Hijutsu*, or secret technique, Musashi only employed it when in an extreme situation, therefore other books featuring tales of great swordsmen do not include this episode in their pages. Only the *Record of the Niten School* preserves this account. Books from later centuries like the *True Record of the Two-Sword School* and *Authoritative Treasury of Martial Arts* contained nothing more than imaginative explanations of what really happened.

In *History of Japanese Kendo* it says,

> *There is a branch of Nito Ryu called On-Ko-Chi-Shin Ryu, the "Study Something Old Learn Something New School." This school is descended from Miyamoto Musashi's Niten Ichi Ryu. It is known colloquially as Gyaku Nito Ryu, Reverse Two-Sword School, because the long sword is held in the left hand and a Tanto is held in the right hand. The Tanto held in the right hand is thrown as a Shuriken and the next move is for the practitioner to rapidly advance and cut with his long sword. However, this tradition has gone extinct and no proper record of it exists.*

前春日の神官高原某、内宮の神官松村平馬この流を授かるといふ記録がある。

と記してゐる。

大日本武德會で發行してゐる『劍道の發達』によれば

……德川時代における二刀流の諸流派は、殆ど皆宮本武藏の二天一流より出でたる末流なり。圓明流、溫故知新流、鐵人流、今枝流の如き卽ちこれなり。その他未來知新流といふが如き二刀流も、聯劍餘談によれば武藏の末流に非ずとあれど（中略）その二刀流の術名に、五輪碎といふものがあるは、武藏の五輪書の名稱を想起せしめ、また極意の飛龍劍と名づくる太刀は、刀を右の手に差しあげて持ち左の手に脇差を振り廻して敵に近づき間を見て短劍を向ふの面に打ちつけて直ちに長劍にて切つて勝つものなるが、この短劍を手裏劍に打つことは、一刀流寶山流などにもあれど武藏の一派圓明流に本來この態を傳ふるのみならず、武藏の最も得意とせし業なりしことより考へ合すれば、この流もまた武藏流の末流と見るをもつて穩當なりとす。

と書いてある。

武藏が、三十五歲前後に、播州龍野城內で、二刀を用ひて、東軍流の使ひ手三宅

That being said, in the Kasuga area of Bizen Domain, the Shinto priest Takahara Something-or-other and a Shinto priest of the inner shrine of Ise Matsumura Heiba are said to have received transmission in Study Something Old Learn Something New School techniques.

In *The Origins and Development of Kendo*, published by the Greater Japan Martial Virtue Society we find the following passage,

Nearly all the many Two-Sword schools that existed in the Tokugawa Era can trace their origins to Miyamoto Musashi's Niten Ichi School, before they diverged off. Some of these schools include Enmei Ryu – Circle of Light School, On-Ko-Chi-Shin Ryu – Study Something Old to Learn Something New School, Tetsujin Ryu – Ironman School and Imaeda Ryu – Now Branch School.[3]

---

[3] The definitions (below) of the schools mentioned above are from the *Dictionary of Martial Arts Schools*:

- *Enmei Ryu – Circle of Light School* This school existed before Miyamoto Musashi and he used this name for his style before changing the name to Niten Ichi Ryu, the Two Heavens as One School.
- *On-Ko-Chi-Shin Ryu – Study Something Old to Learn Something New School* Founded by Kawasumi Heikuro who was taught Chishin School Shuriken.
- *Tetsujin Ryu – Ironman School* Also known as Tetsujin Jitte Ryu, founded by Aoki Kaneie. He studied under Shinmen Muni, Miyamoto Musashi's adopted father and also under Miyamoto Musashi.
- *Imaeda Ryu – Now Branch School* Founded by Imaeda and has sword, staff, Jutte and half-staff techniques.

Later on schools like Chishin Ryu, the Renewed Knowledge School, as well as others had two-sword techniques in their curriculum, however according to <u>A Collection of Stories about Sword Fighting</u>, the Renewed Knowledge School school does not originate from a school based on Miyamoto Musashi's teachings.

Section omitted

There is a technique in this school known as Gorin Kudaki, Breaking the Five Rings, which took its inspiration from Musashi's Book of Five Rings. Also in the technique known as Hiryu Ken, Flying Dragon Sword, the practitioner holds a Katana up in his right hand and a Wakizashi, short sword, in his left. The practitioner waves his Wakizashi around and around. As the opponent draws close, he throws his Wakizashi at the opponent's face. This is followed immediately by a cut with the longs sword, thereby achieving victory. This method of throwing a short sword as a Shuriken can also be found in Itto Ryu and Hozan Ryu.

So this technique, which originates from Musashi's Circle of Light School, is not exclusive to that school. Since this technique, which we can only describe as Musashi's specialty, is also found in Chishin Ryu, the Renewed Knowledge School, it is not unreasonable to categorize Chishin Ryu as being descended from Musashi's teachings.

Translator's Note:
This is the entry for the Chishin School from the *Dictionary of Martial Arts Schools* published 1963:

● Chishin Ryu – Renewed Knowledge School. Shuriken, Naginata and Sword. Founded in the Genwa Era by a man from the Ise region, Ijima Hira Hyoei. He learned Nito Sei Ryu sword fighting from Takemura Youemon and achieved enlightenment to the inner mysteries of Shuriken and Naginata. The tradition was passed down in the Bishu and Seishu regions.

● Takemura Ryu – Bamboo Village School. Shuriken. Founded by Takemura Youemon. An adopted child of Takemura Musashi the name Miyamoto Musashi took while in Edo.

In addition, the *Great Japan Martial Arts Lineage,* published 1982, contains the following passage, which more directly connects Chishin School to Miyamoto Musashi's teachings:

Chishin Ryu was taught in Owari Domain, present day Aichi Prefecture, and was founded by Ijima Ichihyoei...According to a Densho from December of 1828 the founder is considered by many to be another name for a practitioner of Enmei School Kenjutsu, Yada Kuro Uemon. Thus the following lineage can be established:

Miyamoto Musashi
⇩
Takemura Youemon
⇩
Hayashi Ichiro Uemon
⇩
Yada Kuro Uemon ⇨ Ijima Ichihyoei (Chishin School)

End Note

軍兵衞ほか三名を破つたこと、五十三歳ごろに名古屋城內で尾州藩の武藝者を二刀で破り、次いで信州松本城內で、松平直政の家臣及び直政自身と仕會つて、同じくその妙術を發揮したなどの記錄も殘つてゐる。

さて、有名な船島の佐々木小次郎との決鬪であるが、この時の狀況については、『二天記』『武藝小傳』『擊劍叢談』『肥後沼田家記』『古老茶話』『鈴林屑言』『見聞談叢』『武將感狀記』(又、碎玉話)その他の古書ことごとくが、各々異說を記し、その實否是非全く判斷に迷ふの有樣であるが、小次郎は長刀を用ひ武藏は木刀をもつて、遂に打ち勝つたといふことだけは共通である。

著者が、これらの記錄を仔細に熟讀玩味した後の感想としては、『見聞談叢』『武將感狀記』中の一部がどうも專實であるやうに思へてならない。それには、木戟を投げたといふことが載せられてあるからである。

「武藏は、船頭から櫂を請うて二つに割り、手もとを削つて、長いのを二尺五寸、短いのを一

30

Either the year before or the year after Musashi turned 35, he used his two-sword technique to defeat a master of the Togun School named Mitake Gunbe as well as three other Samurai inside the walls of Ryuno Castle in Banshu Domain, present day Hyogo Prefecture. When Musashi was around 35 years old he fought another set of duels inside Nagoya Castle and defeated a martial artist form Oshu Domain with his two-sword style.

Next, in Matsumoto Caste in Shinshu Domain, he fought not only a retainer of Matsudaira Naomasa but also Naomasa himself. The records that remain state Musashi employed his sublime technique to defeat them both.

Descriptions of the famous battle on Boat Island, against Sasaki Kojiro can be found in the *Record of the Niten School, A Short History of All Martial Arts, Tales of Sword Duels, Record of the Numada Family of Higo Domain, Ancient Tales Told over Tea, Kenrin Shigen, Tales of What Was Seen and What Was Heard* and *Record of Samurai Generals' Impressions* (also known as the *Shattered Sphere Talks.)*

Each of these books contains its own differing version of events. Separating truth from falsehood and fact from fiction is nearly impossible, however there are two points all the accounts agree on. The first is that Kojiro wielded a Katana of great length and the second is that Musashi carried only a Bokken, wooden sword, which he struck Kojiro down with.

I, the author, have perused each of these accounts and my impression is that one section found in both *Tales of What Was Seen and What Was Heard* as well as *Record of Samurai Generals' Impressions* rings of truth. The section I am speaking of is when Musashi throws a Ki-hoko, a wooden spear.[4]

---

[4] The following page lists the details for all the books Naruse Sensei mentions in this passage.

- 二天記
Record of the Niten School
by Toyoto Kagehide
1778

- 武芸小伝
Short History of All Martial Arts
By Hinatsu Shigetaka
1714

- 撃剣叢談
Tales of Sword Duels
By Mikami Mototatsu
1790

- 肥後沼田家記
Record of the Numada Family of Higo
By Numada Engen
1672

- 古老茶話
Ancient Tales Told over Tea
By Kashiwazaki Eii
1760

- 鈴林卮言
Kenrin Shigen
Hirayama Kozo
Around 1820

- 見聞談叢
Tales of What Was Seen and What Was Heard
Itoh Baiu
Around 1740

- 武将感状記
Record of Samurai Generals' Impressions
Kumazawa Shotaro
1716

Illustration by Kuniyoshi showing Miyamoto Musashi and Sasaki Kojiro fighting on Boat Island, which became known as Ganryu Island.

手裏剣

尺八寸につくり、舟から上つて岸流（小次郎）と相闘つた。岸流の刀は三尺餘で、武藏はこの時大小の木刀を兩手に持つてかゝると、岸流は先づ拜み打ちに出で、眞向から斬りつけたのを、武藏は左手の大で受け外し、右手の小を、頭目がけて打ちつけたところが、岸流は身を振つてよけたので、それが肩にあたつた。そのはずみに合せて岸流は踏み込み、長刀で横に拂ふと、武藏は尾を縮めて飛び上つたので、皮袴の裾三寸ばかりを切られた。しかしこれと同時に武藏は全力をこめ、諸手をもつて岸流の頭を打つたから、頭は微塵となつて砕け即座に死んだ。」

と、かう書いてある。

春山和尚の記した碑文に、

「或ひは眞劍を飛ばし」とあるを、宍戸梅軒との場合にあてはめて、「或ひは木戟を投げ」とあるを、この佐々木小次郎との場合にあてはめて考へて見ると、不思議に一致するところからも、それと頷けるのである。

かうした事實から、宍戸との場合は、手裏劍で敵の胸を貫き、次の動作で眞向を割り、佐々木との場合は、木戟を敵の肩にあてゝ、次の動作で眞向を砕いたといふ、

The duel is described as follows:

Musashi asked the captain of the boat to give him an oar, which he broke in two. He further trimmed the two pieces by hand until he had a long piece 2 Shaku 5 Sun, 75 centimeters, and a short piece 1 Shaku 8 Sun, 54 centimeters. Musashi rode the boat to meet Ganryu (Sasaki Kojiro) for his duel. Ganryu met Musashi holding a Katana that was 3 Shaku, 90 centimeters, in length while Musashi held a wooden sword in each hand, one long, one short.

The battle began and Ganryu raised his sword high above his head in a two-handed grip and cut straight down at the opponent in front of him. Musashi met and knocked this attack aside with his long wooden sword, held in his left hand. He aimed a cut to the top of Ganryu's head with his short wooden sword, held in his left hand. However, Ganryu moved his body out of the way and the blow missed his head, striking Ganryu's shoulder instead. Ganryu, continuing the movement he started to avoid the cut, stepped forward and sliced horizontally across Musashi's middle with his long sword. Musashi leapt straight up, pulling his legs in close and Ganryu's sword sliced 9 centimeters off the bottom of his Hakama. At the same time Musashi gathered all his strength and struck Ganryu on the head with both swords. Ganryu's head exploded open and he died instantly.

If you recall the *Abbreviated Record* inscription on the Kokura Monument, written by the priest Shunzan, it states,

He also threw swords

We should see this line as referring to Musashi's battle with Shishido Baiken. The following line states,

He threw wooden spears

We should see this line as referring to the battle with Sasaki Kojiro. I don't think these are unreasonable assumptions and I am leaning towards this line of interpretation.

Looking at things this way, Musashi handled the situation with Shishido Baiken by throwing a Shuriken into his enemy's chest and using his next movement to cut straight down. When battling Sasaki Kojiro, Musashi struck his shoulder with a wooden spear and in the next move split him open with a direct strike.

This illustration is from *Record of Miyamoto Musashi's Life* 宮本武蔵一代記 by Tunashima Kamekichi 綱島亀吉. Published 1881.

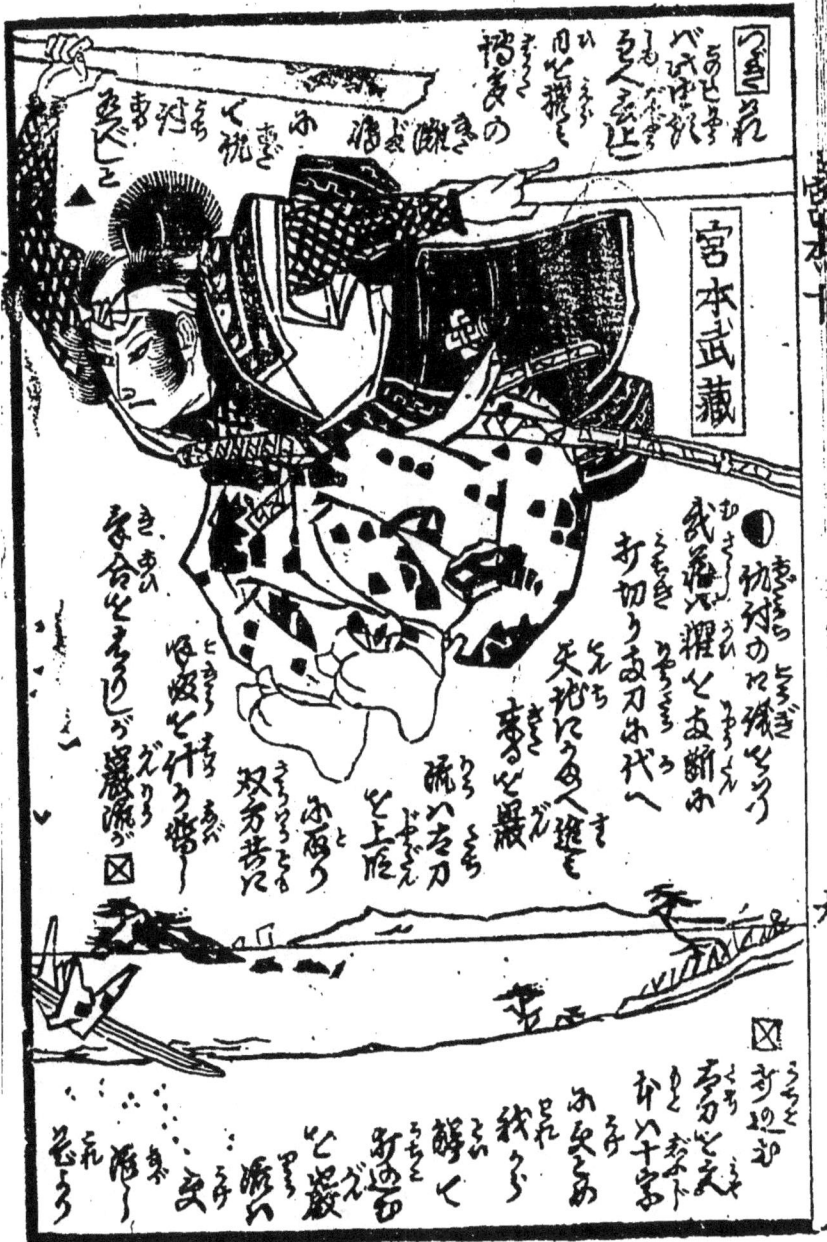

It shows Musashi with two pieces of broken oar, Sasaki Ganryu slicing the bottom of Musashi's Hakama, and Ganryu reeling from a blow to the head.

ほゞ同じ動作の「形」（かた）が得られるのであるが、この形は、根岸流手裏剣術の中の、刀術併用の形となつて今に殘つてゐる。卽ち、一は左手の大刀を前方に垂直に差出して右手に手裏剣を構へ、一は左手の大刀を片手上段にかざして同斷、一は左手の大刀を前方へ向けて同斷、一は左手で大刀を右脇に構へて同斷、而して手裏剣を打ち終ると等しく、右手を大刀に持ち添へて八相にとる動作である。これは武藏が宍戸梅軒の鎖鎌を破つた時の形及び其の應用だと明かに云ひ傳へられてゐる。

以上で、宮本武藏の二刀流なるものゝ起源と經過とが、ほゞ分明するわけであつて、單なる切り込み突つ込みから起つたわざでなかつたことゝは、たしかに斷言出來る。

武藏が後に書いた『兵法三十五ヶ條』『五輪書』中には二刀の理由を、「大刀を片手に取り習はせんため。」と、簡單に述べてあるが、武術の眞の秘奧などは、決して文字に現はさなかつた時代のことだから、すべてをありのまゝに信ずべきでないとは勿論である。

Basically for both of these battles Musashi used the same Kata, or set of movements. This same Kata has been preserved in the Negishi School of Shuriken. It is a technique that is done in conjunction with the Katana.

A brief outline of the Negishi School techniques based on Musashi's fighting style are as follows:

- In this technique hold the Tachi (long sword) in your left hand vertically out in front of you and stand ready with a Shuriken in your right hand.
- In this technique hold the Tachi in your left hand high above your head in Jodan stance, the rest is the same as the first technique.
- In this technique hold the Tachi in your left hand pointed straight out in front of you, the rest is the same as the first technique.
- In this technique hold the Tachi in your left hand in a right armpit stance, the rest is the same as the first technique.

When doing these techniques, as soon as you throw the Shuriken with your right hand you grip the handle of your sword and go into Haso Kamae, or holding the sword vertically, with the handle near your right armpit. This is clearly the same application and set of movements used by Musashi when he defeated Baiken's chain and sickle.

This ends the section on the origins and development of Musashi's two-sword style. I feel I can unequivocally state that Musashi's technique didn't develop simply from cutting or stabbing with his swords.

Later, when Musashi wrote about the principles of his two-sword style in *Thirty-Five Rules for Sword Fighting* 1641 and *The Book of Five Rings* 1645, he says simply "You have to learn how to hold your sword one-handed." In that era, schools of martial arts did not write down specifics about the secret techniques they taught. They assumed most people reading such a book would know there was a lot more to it than words on a page.

剣裏手

武藏の行つた短刀手裏劍といふものが、如何様に打たれたかは、それは傳はつてをらぬが、有名な渡邊幸庵の手記にある『幸庵對話』の中に、

……予は（幸庵自身の事）柳生但馬守宗矩弟子にて免許印可も取たり。竹村武藏（幸庵は常に武藏のことをかく呼んでゐる。）といふ者あり。自己に剣術を錬磨して名人なり。但馬（柳生但馬守のこと）に比べては碁にていへば井目も武藏強し。細川越中守忠興に客人分にて四十人扶持合力あるなり（現米四十人扶持は當時にて草高三百石に相當）子を（養子か、または弟子か）竹村與右衛門といひて、これも武藏について武藝に達す。云々。

……竹村武藏、子は與右衛門といひけり。父に劣らず剣術の名人にて、その上手裏劍の上手なり。川に桃を浮かべて一尺三寸の劍にて打つに、桃の實の核を貫きたり。云々。

かうした記述と、二天記にある宍戸梅軒を打つた記述その他から考へ合せて見ると、廻轉する打ち方ではなくて、弓の矢のやうに眞直に目的物を貫く〝直打〟であつた事と思はれる。

此の〝短刀打ち〟といふ事は、戰國時代末期の戰場武術であり、また一般にも流

40

Unfortunately, Musashi did not leave any writings behind describing the nature of his knife-as-Shuriken technique, however the *Record of Koan* contains the following passage,

I (Koan is referring to himself) received Menkyo Inka, or certification in full transmission, of Shin Kage School sword fighting from Yagyu Tajima no Kami Munenori. There was a man by the name of Takemura Musashi (Koan refers to Miyamoto Musashi by this name.) He was quite famous for having developed and refined his own Kenjutsu, sword art. When compared to Tajima (referring to Yagyu Tajima no Kami,) Musashi was far more adept at Seimoku, the nine principal points in a game of Go. He was an honored guest of Hosokawa Echichu no Kami Tadaoki and had been granted a stipend to support 40 men. (At the time a stiped enough for 40 men meant that Musashi's total renumeration was around 300 Koku, 300 bales of rice.) His child (possibly an adopted child or a disciple/ student) was named Takemura Yoemon. Yoemon was a dedicated follower of Musashi and had developed his marital arts to a high level. And so on and so forth...

...Takemura Musashi's son was a man named Yoemon. His skill in sword fighting was in no way inferior to that of his father's and he was quite well-known. In addition, Yoemon was an expert at Shuriken. He could toss a peach into the river and, with a dagger 1 Shaku 3 Sun, 39 centimeters long, strike it dead center with enough force so that the tip pierced the pit. And so on and so forth.

If we merge what we learned from this account with the account written in the *Record of the Niten School* regarding how Musashi struck down Shishido Baiken, we can see his Shuriken throwing style. It is not Kaiten, revolving style, but Shinchoku, straight style, like an arrow shooting towards its target. Another way to describe it is Choku-uchi, Straight Direct Strike.[5]

---

[5] The *Record of Koan* 1709 was written by Watanabe Koan who supposedly lived from 1582 ~ 1711, making him 128 years old when he died. All the information in brackets is by Naruse Kanji.

行してゐたと見え、馬手差又は右手差と稱する七八寸の短刀を、右手を以て直ちに拔き得る場所へ隱しざしにして置き、戰時には大小の外にこの馬手差を二振も三振も用意した者のあつた事は、戰記類にも見えてゐる。かうした短刀は、反りのない鋭い形で、柄とのつり合をよくとつて置くなど、充分効果的につくられてあり、これで戰つた戰記も相當に多い。

手裏劍といふものは、この直打と、廻轉打との二形式で、廻轉打には、また一廻轉打と多廻轉打との區別がある。

武藏の手裏劍については、もう一つの記錄がある。かれがかつて尾州藩に來往した事については、近松茂矩の『昔咄』に書いてあるが、その時に、この手裏劍を傳へた事が『日本武術名家傳』に載つてゐる。

一、手離劍之事　知新流

手離劍は其名久しく行はれし者なれ共其傳法の有事不詳。尾張藩へ傳へ始めしは丹羽織江氏

This Tanto-uchi, throwing a knife, was a martial technique used on the battlefield in the late Warring States Period of the 16th century. Such knives eventually became popular to carry. The knives were called Medezashi, which could be written as Horse-Directed-by-the Hand or Directed-by-the-Right-Hand, depending on the Kanji used. These were Tanto, knives, 7 or 8 Sun 21~ 24 centimeters long and were meant to be drawn and thrown quickly with your right hand. Thus they were kept in a spot hidden, but easily accessible. In records of military campaigns and the like, it is said that some Samurai would carry two or three Medezashi in addition to their long and short Katana.

These knives were forged straight, not curved like Katana. Medezashi had straight blades that came to a sharp point with a close fitting handle and other features. They were crafted for maximum efficiency and I was able to find many accounts of their use in records of military campaigns.

There are two different ways of throwing Shuriken. Choku-uchi, Straight Throw, and Kaiten-uchi, Revolving Throw. In addition, there are two sub-categories of Revolving Throw: One Revolution Throw and Multiple Revolution Throw.

There is another reference to Musashi and Shuriken. A Samurai named Chikamatsu Shigenori wrote a book called *Tales From Long Ago* written in 1738, that contained an account of Shuriken. This book was included in *Tales of Famous Japanese Martial Arts Families* published in 1902, and I have included that entry here.

On the Topic of Shuriken
Chishin Ryu, The Renewed Knowledge School

Shuriken throwing is an art that has been practiced by many people since days of old, though there is no information regarding its origins or development.

張也。傍背に氏張は中頃宮本武藏の弟子に竹村與右衞門と云ふ者有り。其弟子に飯島平兵衞と云ふ者あり。此人工夫して飯島源太左衞門、日置重右衞門、淺野傳右衞門等へ段々傳へて、同人より、丹羽織江氏張が傳授を受けしとあり。此術は甲冑に身を固め二間柄の槍を携へたる敵に向つて施すべき術に非ず。道中旅行の節山賊等の類に出合し時に先を打て進み退ける器なりと云へり。乍然手離劍にて必ず一人を打倒すものと思ふべからず。人は一双一突にて死する者に非ず。玆に一二の例をあぐれば、鎌倉の橫五郎景政は十三束三ツ伏弓三人張にて眼を射られしも、物の數ともせず、忠慶は左の腕を打落されても組討し、又丹羽左京太夫の臣成田彌右衞門と云ふ者、秀吉公の爲め礫に懸られし時、七所突かれても空死し、其夜郎黨來りてはりつけ柱をおろし助けたりと武備目睫記にも見えたり。右の成田常に語りて云ふ、勇者は膽にさへ疵付ずば體はみぢんに成つても容易に死すべき者にあらず。我此度礫に行はる〻とも膽さへ突れざれば必ず死せず。夜に來ておろして介抱すべしと云ひ置し言の如し。去ば勇者は弓鎗太刀にても容易に死せざる者也。

手裏劍にて即死させんとは不覺なる事なるべし。唯先を打て其虛に乘じて勝を得るには良器たるべし。

　　　知新流、手離劍系圖

The first person to teach these techniques in Owari Domain was Tanba Orie Ujiharu. According to Ujiharu's documents when Miyamoto Musashi was in his middle years he had a disciple named Takemura Youemon. His disciple was a man called Ijima Heibe. He developed many ingenious methods and passed his teaching to Ijima Tasaemon, Heii Shigeuemon, Asano Denuemon and so on until the aforementioned Tanba Orie Ujiharu received transmission of the teachings.

Shuriken throwing not the kind of technique you would use against a Samurai in full armor carrying a spear with a 4 meter long handle. Instead it is something you would use to defend yourself against brigands or other ruffians while walking down a trail through the forest. You would throw a Shuriken before either retreating or advancing. This is what Shuriken are for. That being said, you should not think of the Shuriken as a weapon that can be counted on to topple an opponent. People can't be killed with a single stab wound. Allow me to give one or two examples here.

Kamakura Gongoro Kagemasa (1069 ~ ?) was shot with an arrow from a bow twelve fists long and three fingers wide right in the eye but continued to fight.

Tadakei (unknown) had his left arm chopped off but continued to grapple on the battlefield.

Further, a retainer of Tanba Ukyotaifu named Narita Jiuemon, was crucified on the orders of Lord Hideyoshi. He was stabbed seven times with spears and left for dead. However, according to The Eyelashes (Secrets) of War Preparation 1739 that night his companions took him down from the cross and were able to save him.

The above was all related by Narita Tsune. He emphasized that brave warriors do not have the slightest crack in their livers (their martial spirit,) even if their bodies are pulverized they somehow fail to die.

This applies to us as well. If we are strapped to a crucifix and stabbed through the liver, we will not die. Remember at night someone will come and take you down and bind your wounds. In conclusion brave warriors are not easy to kill, whether by bow, spear or sword.

○某　飯島平兵衞　同源太左衞門　某　日置重右衞門　重長　淺野傳右衞門　氏張　丹羽織江

ちよつと前後するが、宮本武藏と尾州藩との關係の異説とも見らるべきものが、同じく同書に載せてある。

あまり流布してゐないだけに、珍とすべき事の一つであらう。

二刀兵法の尾州に始る事は、無二流山田左近太夫盛次を以始めとす。盛次門人に彥坂八兵衞忠重と云者有。此術に達す。後に宮本武藏が門弟となり、其後又竹村與右衞門と云ふ者尾州へ來り、時に忠重竹村に隨ひ武藏正流想道圓明の兵法を究む。其頃の門弟林不善翁と云者有。其子林市郎左衞門資就と云（父子ともに武藏の弟子）なり。賢き二刀遣ひ成りしが、竹村來りし時、又是に從ひて書傳を受け、故に此人の業は武藏より父不善に傳、理は竹村より傳ると云へり。是を八田九郎右衞門知義先生圓流に授く、知義此術を以て大に名を鳴す。武助の門弟にて出傑なる者は岩間武太夫安綱邦俊、石黑善太夫信久其傳を繼て門下に指南す。其後左右田武助馬場市右衞門信備、丹羽織江氏張、左右田與平邦正等、後に各門弟を取立る。兹に故有て左右田邦俊の子孫斷絶に付、市川六郎左衞門長之此師範を相續す。

You should dismiss the notion that Shuriken are something that can kill someone instantaneously. They are a tool that allow you to launch an initial strike that your opponent will mistake for your main attack. As he responds to that lie, you achieve victory with your true attack.

Lineage of the Chishin School of Shuriken

Common Name Unknown Ijima Hira Hyoei
⇩
Common Name Unknown Ijima Genta Saemon
⇩
Common Name Unknown Heki Shige Uemon
⇩
Shigenaga Asano Den Uemon
⇩
Ujihari Tanba Orie

There is another interesting passage from *Tales From Long Ago* giving a different account of Miyamoto Musashi's time in Oshu Domain. I'm not sure if this should have been placed before or after the last section but since this book is difficult to come by, I will share this curious passage here.

Nito Ryu, Two-Sword School, was first taught in Oshu by a master of Muni School Yamata Ukin Tayu Moritsugi. His teachings were passed onto a disciple of Moritsugi named Hikosaka Hachibe Tadashige. He became an expert in this art. Later he became a discipline of Miyamoto Musashi. Sometime after that, a man by the name of Takemura Youemon came to Oshu and eventually both Tadashige and Takemura trained until they had reached the pinnace of Musashi Sei Ryu, the Musashi True School, as well as Sodo Enmei no Heiho, Path of Thought Circle of Light Way of the Sword. Around this time there was a disciple named Hayashi Fuzeno. His son was Hayashi Ichiro Saemon Motonari (Both father and son were disciples of Musashi.) They both trained in the two-sword style diligently and with insight.

When Takemura arrived he too followed their example, eventually gaining certification in Musashi's art. Due to their prowess Musashi eventually granted the father, Fuzeno, transmission of the techniques and to Takemura he granted transmission of the principles

Later Hatta Kurouemon Tomoyoshi Sensei became the head of Enmei Ryu, Circle of Light School, and Tomoyoshi was able to make himself famous with what he had learned. Later, Souda Takesuke Kunitoshi and Ishikuro Zendayu Nobuhisa codified the teachings and taught them to the other students. Among Takesuke's premiers students Iwama Budayu Yasutsuna, Baba Ichiuemon Nobumitsu, Tanba Orie Ujiharu, Souda Yohei Kunimasa.

Each of these students later helped the other students to excel. The reason that Ichikawa Rokuro Saemon Nagayuki became the succeeding Shihan, or head instructor, is because Souda Takesuke Kunitoshi's descendants all died out.

Translator's Note:

According to the *Dictionary of Martial Arts Schools* Muni Ryu, the school of Miyamoto Musashi's father, taught Jutte, a metal truncheon, or sword breaker. Muni Ryu also contained sword and Kyoho "Strong Way" a kind of Koppo or method of striking the vital points and using joint manipulation. Muni Ryu was founded by a student of Miyamoto Musashi named Aoki Tsune Uemon. This school is descended from Miyamoto Munisai's Tori School which consisted of Sword, Kogusoku (Jujutsu, fighting with short swords or knives) and Jutte (truncheon.)

剣　裏　手

かうした文献のほかに、物語稗史としての武藏の手裏劍武勇傳は二三ある。その中で伊賀の上野で宍戸を破つた話が諸國に傳はつた頃、程近い大和國柳生庄に在住の柳生石舟齋がこれをきゝ、考ふるところがあつてゝつてを求めて宮本武藏を自邸に招き、件のゝ左手に太刀を、右手に短刀をもち、それを手裏劍に打つ武術と、己れの劍術と立會つたが、三度が三度とも石舟齋が破れた。かれは、殘念に思つたといふよりも、むしろいたく感心して、厚く武藏をもてなし、更に何囘も立合ひを求め專らそれを破る工夫を凝らしたといふ話であつて、流石人間が出來てゐただけに、

石舟齋は、大悟一番、工夫に工夫を重ねて、遂にそれを破り得る事を完成したのが柳生流にある有名な秘傳として、正統柳生子爵家に今も傳はる『活人劍の巻』の十字手裏劍神妙劍がそれであるといはれてゐる。

しかし、これは武藏對石舟齋の關係ではなくて、事實とすれば武藏對柳生但馬守宗矩（石舟齋の子）間の事であつたらうと思はれる。

何故なれば、柳生流が手裏劍に對して工夫したといはるゝ〝無構への構へ〟即ち

Documents like this along with the other historic tales and inscriptions on stone slabs have allowed me to introduce two or three heroic tales of Miyamoto Musashi and his Shuriken art. One of those tales, the defeat of Shishido Baiken in the Ueno region of Iga Domain, soon spread all over Japan.

This story caught the imagination of Yagyu Sekishusai in the relatively nearby Yagyuatsu Region of Yamato Domain. He invited Miyamoto Musashi to his residence and arranged to have a training duel with his sword against Musashi's famous technique. Namely, he wanted to face off against this Musashi who armed himself with a long sword in his right hand and a short sword in his left, which he would throw as a Shuriken. In the end, Sekishusai lost three duels out of three.

However, rather than being dejected by this, Sekishusai was intrigued and paid every courtesy to Musashi, hosting him as an honored guest. It is said he requested duels again and again, each time focusing all his energy on developing a Kufu, knack or trick, that would enable him to defeat this type of attack.

People who completely devote themselves to a task invariably find success and Sekishusai eventually received one of the great inspirations of his life. By struggling to develop a new approach to solve his problem, he eventually discovered a way to defeat Musashi's technique.

The resulting technique became a famous Hiden, or secret teaching, taught in the Yagyu School. Even today, it is still taught in the remaining true lineage Viscount Yagyu family. It is part of the Katsujin *Ken no Maki, Life Giving Sword Scroll* and is titled *Sublime Cross Shaped Sword Response Against Shuriken.* That being said this story probably did not involve Yagu Sekishusai, instead, in all likelihood Musashi's opponent was Yagyu Tajma no Kami Munenori (Sekishusai's son.)

火乱坊ノ圖

手裏劍の飛んで來る先に事を叶へて、十字にそれを切つて落す〝十字手裏劍〟の妙

境から秘奧を得度したのがこの宗矩であ

り、石舟齋が八十歲の高齡で慶長十一年に

歿した時に、武藏は二十二歲、宗矩は、武

藏に十三歲の年長者であつた等の諸點から

考へてさう思へるのである。

話は少しわきみちに外れるが、有名な上

泉秀綱の劍法「新陰流」の秘傳中にも、こ

の〝短刀打劍〟の術があつて同流最古の文

献である慶長十五年の新陰流目錄中にはす

でにかうした二刀流の形が圖示してある。

その中の『天狗書卷』にある、火亂房とい

ふ法體が、知羅天といふ烏天狗と立會つてる圖を見るに、天狗は一刀、それに對向

52

The man from the Yagyu school who solved the problem of how to defeat a Shuriken with *The Stance of No Stance* was Munenori, Sekishusai's son. In this technique you hold your swords in a Juji, or cross shape, to stop Shuriken thrown at you by an opponent. Munenori was the one that drew from the mysterious otherworld the technique of cutting a cross in response to an opponent throwing a Shuriken and enshrined it in the secret teachings of the Yagyu School.

At the time Yagyu Sekishusai was quite advanced in years. When he died in the 11th year of Keicho (1606) he was 80 years old. Musashi was around 22 at the time and Munenori was only 13 years his senior. Looking at things objectively, it is clear that this story tells of how Munenori faced off against Musashi.

This may be going off on a tangent, however Yagyu Sekishusai was taught Kage School sword fighting by Kamiizumi Hidezuna. Within that school there is a secret technique called Tanto Uchi Ken, Throwing the Sword Like a Knife. In a Shinkage School document dating from the 15th year of Keicho, there is an illustration of a two-sword technique. The document is called Shinkage Ryu Mokuroku, a *Catalogue of Techniques from the New Shadow School*, and within that there is a sub-section called *The Tengu Scroll*. The illustration shows a Buddhist priest-like figure labeled Hiranbo, Wildfire Monk, facing off against a Tengu, a mountain goblin, with bird-like features called Chiraten.

The Tengu is armed with a single Katana while the Buddhist priest-like figure has two swords.

The illustration shows him with the short sword in his right hand and the long sword in his left hand. This stance is called Gyaku-Nito, Reverse Two-Sword, since the typically the long sword would be held in the dominant right hand.

劍裏手

する法體は二刀――右手に短刀左手に長刀といふ逆二刀の圖形を顯示し、しかもその右手の短刀をまさに投げんとする體勢を現はしてをり、一方の天狗もそれに對應する俊敏な身のこなしである。

柳生流中興の祖である但馬守宗嚴卽ち石舟齋が、當時諸國を廻國して大和の國を訪れた上泉秀綱について、その秘奥を學び皆傳を得た事は有名な話で、多分さうした不思議な二刀流を破る事が出來ず、後に工夫して秀綱を驚嘆させたのであるとも思はれる。

かくて「十字手裏劍」の原型が宗矩に傳はり、宗矩が宮本武藏の手裏劍と立會つて、一層それを深刻化したものと考へてよい。もつとも、これを工夫完成したのは大阪の毛利玄達の手裏劍と仕合つた結果だと一般に云ひ傳へられてゐるし、またさう思はれる節々が十分にある。

さて、最初に戻つて、小倉の城主小笠原侯の家老として仕へた、宮本武藏の養子

Further, the illustration depicts the right hand holding the short sword is readying to throw. In opposition to this the Tengu is readying to respond deftly and nimbly to such an attack.

While travelling around Japan Kamiizumi Hidetsuna, who later changed his name to Kamiizumi Nobutsuna encountered the man who re-invigorated the Yagyu School, Tajma no Kami Muneyoshi also known as Sekishusai. It is a well-known story that Sekishusai studied with Kamiizumi until he became enlightened to the inner secrets of Shinkage Ryu and received Kaiden, complete transmission, of all the techniques and philosophy of the New Shadow School.

It seems likely that though Sekishusai was unable to defeat this mysterious two-sword school of Miyamoto Musashi. Sekishusai's later discovery of an imaginative counter would no doubt have astounded Hidezuna. Later, the rough form of Juji Shuriken, A Cross Shaped Cut Against a Shuriken, was passed down to Munenori and it was Munenori that dueled with Musashi and his Shuriken. This directly resulted in the technique becoming more developed, though it was not completed until after the duel against the Shuriken technique of Mori Gentatsu of Osaka. While this is not definitively the reason word of this marvelous technique spread, it certainly seems the most likely one.[6]

---

[6] Mori Gentatsu was a woman who dressed as a man and travelled around the country training in martial arts. She was the head of Mori School Shuriken. There are many novels about her but no real records of her other than one mentioning she took part in a great martial arts exhibition in Edo in 1632. The event was in front of the Emperor and featured martial artists from all over Japan. Mori Gentatsu defeated Yoshioka Matasaburo of the Yoshioka School of Kodachi short sword with her Shuriken. Her next opponent was Yagyu Munenori or possibly his son Yagyu Jube Mitsuyoshi (1607-1650.) She began to throw Shuriken at him, but he deflected them all with his wooden sword. Disheartened she challenged him to use a smaller weapon and he switched to his Tessen, iron fan. She was still unable to defeat him. There are some Japanese novels that feature Yagyu Jubei and Mori Gentatsu travelling around Japan together.

伊織（甥とも從弟ともいはれてゐる。）が、内々の君命も手傳ひ、かた〴〵武藏の死後十年目の承應三年にその碑をたてた事について、著者の新しい發見を述べて見よう。

武藏の養子伊織は、慶長十七年十月二十一日、播州印南郡米田村に生れ、寛永三年十五歳の時、當時播州明石十萬石の城主小笠原大學頭忠眞に奉仕した。忠眞は、寛永九年十一月、十七萬石となつて豐前國小倉城に移り、後二萬石を子孫に分封して明治維新に至つたのであるが、養子伊織の縁で、武藏はこの忠眞の下に寛永十一年ごろから、熊本の細川侯に仕へた十七年八月まで、七年間滯在してゐた事實がある。その原因理由については、たゞ、養子伊織との縁による、といふより外に書かれたり語られたりしてはをらぬが、著者は、單刀直入に、これは「手裏劍による縁だ。」と斷言したい。

甚だ唐突のやうだが、小倉の城主當時右近太夫忠眞が、短刀打の手裏劍の名手であつた事は已に述べたところである。最初は忠政といひ、後に忠眞と改名した。大

So then, returning to the beginning, Miyamoto Musashi's adopted son Iori (some stories say Iori was his nephew and others his cousin) served as an elder advisor to the Lord Ogasawara of Kokura Castle. He was a personal assistant to the lord with regular contact. In the 3rd year of Sho-o (1654) ten years after Musashi died they erected the Kokura Musashi memorial stone. With regards to this plinth the author has made a new discovery, and I would like to share that with you.

Musashi's adopted son Iori was born on September 21st in the 17th year of Keicho (1612) in Banshu Domain In-nangun Komeda Village. In the 3rd year of Kanei (1626) at the age of 15 he entered the service of the lord of the castle Ogasawara Daigakugashira Tadazane, who at the time had a 100,000 Koku stipend. Tadazane's stipend was increased to 170,000 Koku in the 9th year of Kanei (1632) and he moved to Kokura Castle in Bizen Domain. He later divided his estate into 20,000 Koku fiefs and granted them to his decedents. These estates continued until the Meiji Restoration in 1868. What this means is since Miyamoto Musashi was the adopted son of Iori Musashi, he was able to obtain a position serving Tadazane from around the 11th year of Kanei (1634.) Musashi served lord Hosokawa of Kumamoto for seven years until August the of the 17th year of Kanei (1640.)

However, the reason for Musashi was employed goes beyond the connection with his adopted son, Iori. While this is not written in any form anywhere, this writer will say simply and directly that the connection is Shuriken. While this may seem like a shot in the dark I have already stated that the lord of Kokura Castle at the time Ukon Taiyu Tadazane was an expert at Shuriken. Originally his name was Tadamasa, but he later changed it to Tadazane.

手裏劍

阪の陣には、忠政は、當時信州深志（今の松本）の城主たりし父信濃守能政、兄忠脩と共に出陣し、父兄共に戰死したので、忠政はその遺領を相續したものであるが、この忠政もすでに危ふかつたところを、かねて手練の手裏劍で危機を脱したのであつたから、後に平和になつてからも、手裏劍術への執心は一層ふかく、幾通りもの劍を工夫し、わざ〳〵侍臣をつかはして長船祐定一派に鍛へさせ、常にその修錬を怠らなかつたといふ話も殘つてゐる。

徳川三代將軍家光の治世に、千代田の殿中では妙な事が流行した。伊達政宗が木刀をさし、加賀の前田は金無垢の長煙管をさし、小笠原探題は（忠眞の事）黑がね作りの短刀樣の物に穴をあけ、朱の總をつけたものを、鞘なしでさしてゐたといふ事を『日本隨筆大成』で讀んだ。

思ふに、それは忠眞の發明になる〝特殊な手裏劍〞であつたらうと領かれることは、東京市小石川區林町の元の一橋家である徳川伯爵家御所藏の數多い手裏劍の中

Tadazane participated in the Siege of Osaka, the series of battles between the Tokugawa and the Toyotomi that lasted from 1614 ~ 1615. He entered battle with his elder brother Tadanaga and father Hidemasa, who was at the time the lord of Fukashi Castle (present day Matsumoto Castle) in Shinshu Domain. Both his elder brother and father were killed in the battle and Tadazane inherited the title and lands.

However, during that battle Tadazane faced a perilous situation and he was only able to extricate himself from by using his well-practiced Shuriken skills. Thus, even as Japan began the peaceful Edo Era, his dedication to the Shuriken arts only increased.

Tadazane made many refinements to his sword and went out of his way to send attendants to the Osafune Sukesada School, the great swordsmiths of Bizen Domain, to have one forged to his specifications. It is said he was never negligent when it came to training, and continually refined his Shuriken technique.

During the peaceful reign of the third Tokugawa Shogun Iemitsu, many strange things came into fashion at the imperial court at Chiyoda. Date Masamune went about with a Bokken, wooden sword, in his belt, Kaga no Maeda had a long solid gold Kiseru pipe in his belt, and Ogasawara Tandai (referring to Tatazane) had an iron knife-like blade in his belt. The blade had a hole drilled in it and a crimson tassel threaded through the hole. He kept it wedged in his belt without a scabbard. This can all be found in the pages of *Great Collection of Miscellaneous Japanese Writings* 1927.

It is my contention that the weapon described above is the "special Shuriken" invented by Tadazane.[7]

---

[7] *The Osaka Gunki* Record of the Osaka Campaign contains the line, 小笠原忠政、敵に胸板と肌との間を鑓にて突き返されたるが、忠政脇差を抜きて手裏剣に打ちたるに、敵ひるんで鑓を抜きたるによりて命助かりたり『大阪軍記』

An enemy soldier stabbed at Ogasawara Tadamasa (Tadazane) with a spear, which went in between his breastplate and his skin. Tadamasa drew his Wakizashi short sword and threw it like a Shuriken. The enemy fell away and he was able to pull out the spear and survive.

A Tanto knife-shaped Shuriken used by Ogasawara Tadazune.

（長さ）八寸　（元幅）八分五厘　（棟厚み）五分　（重畳）七十匁

（藏氏敬宗川德爵伯）

A Shuriken owned by Count Tokugawa Muneyoshi (1897 ~ 1989)

Length :	8 Sun 24 centimeters
Width at the base :	5 Bun 5 Ri 1.7 centimeters
Width of the spine :	5 Bun1.5 centimeters
Weight :	70 Monme 265 grams

手裏劍叢談

に、長さ八寸元幅八分五厘、棟の厚み五分、重量七十匁、どうみても、鎧通しの中心を切つたといふやうな形の、基部から二寸位のところに穴をあけ、赤褐色の絹糸の總のついたもののあるのを眞の用ひたものゝ模造であるよつたら、これがその忠

武藏が、手裏劍への執心者忠眞の許に食客として數年間滯在したといふ原因は、大略かくの如き事情であつたことと信ずる。

その後の武藏は、寛永十七年に、熊本の細川忠利から招かれて、その客分となつたのであるが、この細川忠利の夫人は、小笠原忠眞の實妹で、一旦徳川秀忠將軍の養女となつて江戸城から細川家へ嫁入りしたもので、さうした關係から、兩者は義兄弟の間柄であつたのだから、その忠眞の推薦で細川家に仕へる事となつたのかも知れない。

、細川家では、はじめ十七人扶持十八石から、三百石を賜はり、こゝで有名な『兵

In the former residence of the Ichibashi household in Tokyo City, Ishikawa Ku, Hayashi Cho holds the Collection of the Count Tokugawa Household. Among the many Shuriken in that collection there is one that has a length of 8 Sun, a width at the base of 5 Bun 5 Ri, a spine width of 5 Bun and a weight of 70 Monme.[8] To me the shape of this Shuriken looks like it has been cut out of a Yoroi-toshi, a multipurpose knife and defensive tool carried by Samurai. About 2 Sun, 6 centimeters, from the base there is a hole and cord of braided reddish-brown silk. Having seen this piece with my own eyes I feel it is the same Shuriken design as the one used by Tadazane.

While the above is nothing more than a rough outline, it is the reason I believe why Musashi ended up being a house guest to Tadazane, a man passionate about Shuriken, for several years.

Later, in the 17th year of Kanei, he became an honored guest of Hosokawa Tadayoshi. Hosokawa Tadayoshi's wife was the older sister of Ogasawara Tadazune. She was previously the adopted daughter of the Shogun Tokugawa Hidetada and when she got married she moved from Edo Castle to the Hosokawa household. Thus both men are brothers-in-law so in all likelihood Tatazune probably recommended Musashi be given a position in the Hosokawa household.

When he first began serving the Hosokawa household Musashi had a salary to support 17 men, about 18 Koku. Later, this was raised to 300 Koku.

---

[8] See the photograph on page 59.

法三十五ヶ條』を書き、更に『五輪書』を完成し、その間、餘技として繪畫を描き金工に耽り、道士らしく行ひすまして、正保二年五月十九日、居る事六年、行年六十二歳にして世を去つたのである。後年その石碑が、熊本城下ならずして、小倉に建立されたのも、そのころまだ小笠原忠眞が健在であつたからの事で、承應三年の建碑にあたつて、特にその碑文中に、武藏の手裏劍術の一項を強調させたのも、また縁由のある事と信じられるのである。

●

Musashi authored the famous *Thirty-five Rules for Sword Fighting* and completed the *Book of Five Rings* while in his service. In the rest of his time he painted pictures did metalwork and otherwise behaved as an ascetic monk.

On May 19th of the 2nd year of Tenpo, after six years of service, Musashi entered the next world after 62 years of life. Later a stone monument was erected, not below Matsumoto Castle but near Kokura. The reason for this is Ogasawara Tadazune was still alive and in good health. It is my belief that the section of the stone monument erected in the 3rd year of Sho-o that emphasizes his Shuriken arts is highly significant.

Tohjutsu Kumi Komi no Kata

Sword and Shuriken Techniques

Naruse Kanji

Translator's Introduction

Tohjutsu Kumi Komi no Kata
Sword and Shuriken Techniques
By Naruse Kanji

In this section Naruse Kanji interprets Musashi's sword and Shuriken technique using Bo-Shuriken, stick-like Shuriken. There are a total of five sword and Shuriken combination techniques.

剣 の 術

刀術組込の形

これはたゞ参考の爲に記述するだけであるから、解説も簡単にする。刀術組込の形又は刀術併用の形といつて、日本刀を以て敵と闘ふ時、どんな具合にして手裏剣を打つかといふ、その形を示したものであつて、全部で五本ある。

このうち、二本目或

（刀　抜）日　本　一

ひは四本目の形は、宮本武藏が、宍戸梅軒の鎖鎌を手裏剣で破つた時の姿から取つ

68

Technique 1
Photograph 1 : Battoh – Drawing the Sword

I am adding this section just to give the reader a clearer idea of the concepts introduced in this book, so the explanations will be simple. There are two terms for these type of techniques,

- Tohjutsu Kumikomi no Kata : Paired Sword (and Shuriken) Attacking Techniques

and

- Tohjutsu Kyoyo no Kata : Techniques Using (Shuriken) in Conjunction With Katana

In other words the following five techniques demonstrate how to throw a Shuriken in different situations while engaging in combat with an enemy using a Japanese sword.

In particular the second technique as well as the fourth technique are inspired by the method Miyamoto Musashi used to defeat Shishido Baiken's Kusari Gama, chain and sickle. These are my interpretations of how Musashi may have won this duel.

たものではないかと想像されて居る。手裏剣は、「不殺削闘剣」といひ、手裏剣を以ては直接に殺さずして單に戰闘力を削ぐにとゞめ、殺す必要があれば、刀を以てするといふのが本來であるから、かうした併用の形も起つた事と思はれる。

此の形は、單に手裏劍術と刀術とを組合せるといふ事だけに過ぎないので、刀を以て斬るといふやうな動作は取り入れてなく手裏劍を打つにしてもそれは、體のこなしと働きとをあらはさんが爲に過ぎないものである事を附記して置く。

一本目（片手八相に）

劍裏手

70

Technique 1
Photograph 2 : Kata Te Haso Ni – Going Into Haso Stance

Shuriken are known as a "Non-Lethal Blade to End A Fight." In other words a weapon that will not result in your opponent's death, but will shave away his will to fight. In other words, if it is necessary to dispatch your opponent you would use your Katana to kill. This is thought to be how Shuriken originated.

These techniques are only meant to demonstrate how Shuriken are used in conjunction with Tohjutsu, Katana techniques. I will not be including any specifics on how to cut with the Katana. Further, the Shuriken throwing pictures are only included to give the reader an idea of how the body moves as the throwing action is done.

手裏劍の術

手裏劍五本を右前牛にたばさみ、日本刀は右手に提げて場に出る。立禮を終つ

て、刀を左手に持ちかへ帶刀、下げ緒からみの後、一本目の形に入るのである。

先づ、左手鞘口を持ち、右手、鍔元五分ばかり離して刀柄を持ち、右足を斜前方

に一尺程踏み出して刀を抜き終ると共に抜いた刀を片手八相にとつて右足をもど

す。即ち柄と右手腕とを併行にして右胸脇に構へ、左手で鞘

一日本）刀を左手に持ちかへ
（右手々手裏劍とを…る）

口を握つたま丶直立して前方の標的に見入るのである。

次に、刀を左に持ちかへて構へ、前方を凝視しつ丶、右手で手裏劍一本をぬき出

して右手に持つ。（持ち終つた手は右下に下げてゐる。）

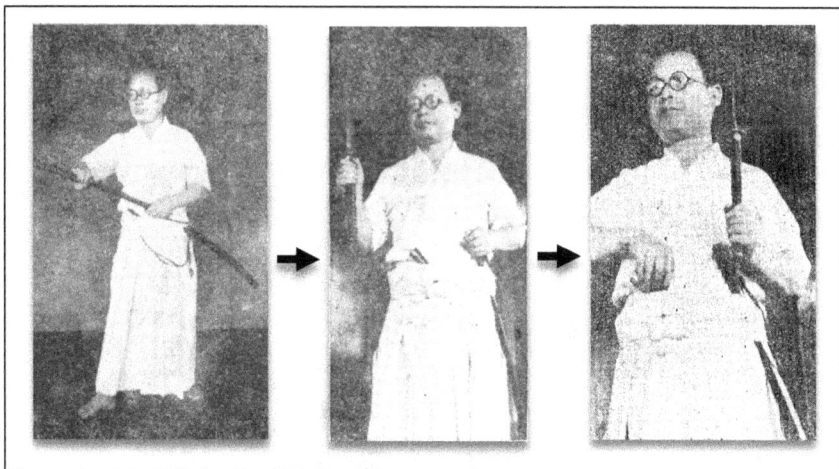

Technique 1
Photograph 3 :
Switching your Katana to your left hand and drawing a
Shuriken with your right hand

Slide five Shuriken into the front of your Hakama so they are held fast. Raise your Japanese sword in your right hand as you step onto the training area. After finishing your standing bow, switch the Katana to your left hand and slide it into your belt and wrap the Sageo, cord tied to the top of your Katana, around the scabbard. Having secured your Katana the first technique begins.

First take hold of the Saya-guchi, mouth of the scabbard – the point the sword meets the scabbard, with your left hand. Place your right hand on the handle of your Katana about 1.5 centimeters above Tsuba-moto, the sword guard. Step diagonally forward with your right foot 1 Shaku, 30 centimeters. When you finish drawing your Katana move to a one-handed Haso stance and step back with your right foot to your starting position. At this point you should be standing facing your opponent with the handle of the sword in your right hand, with your right arm pulled towards the right side of your chest and your left hand gripping the opening of your scabbard.

Next, switch the Katana to your left hand as you stare forcefully straight at your opponent. With your right hand draw out one Shuriken and hold it in your right hand. (When you finish drawing a Shuriken allow your right hand to hang by your side.)

刀を左片手上段に、手裏剣を規定の如くに構へ、左半身となつて、じりじりと敵に迫る。此の時の呼吸が非常に大切なものであつて、「陰にともる」といふのである。

左上段に構へた刀は、左上

（片手上段の構へ）日本一

それより、標的に向つて数歩歩み寄り、程よき間合を以て、「ヤッ」と一聲氣合を聲にとめると共に、左手の

（一）前直の刀納

（瞬間）日本一刀て八相に打ち終る）つるに相

241

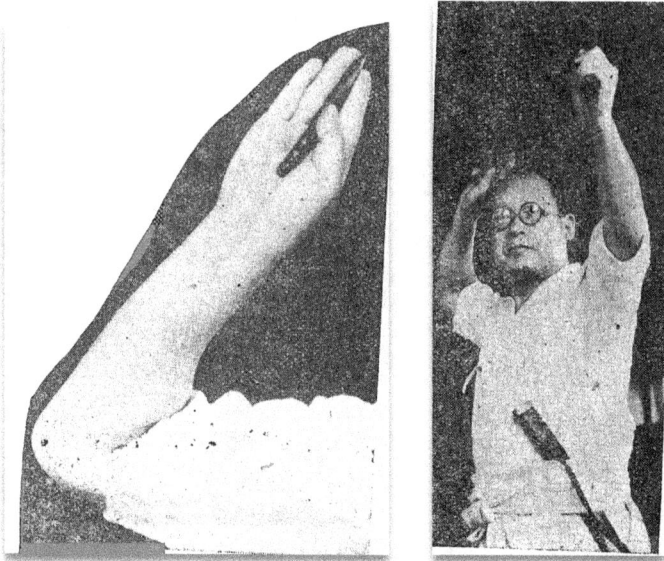

Technique 1
Photograph 4 : One-handed Jodan Kame

Next, take several strides towards your opponent and, when you have reached an appropriate distance shout a Kiai of Ya! And raise the Katana in your left hand up into Jodan stance, with the sword above your head. Raise your right hand with the Shuriken held in the proper way, and your body twisted so your left side is towards your opponent.

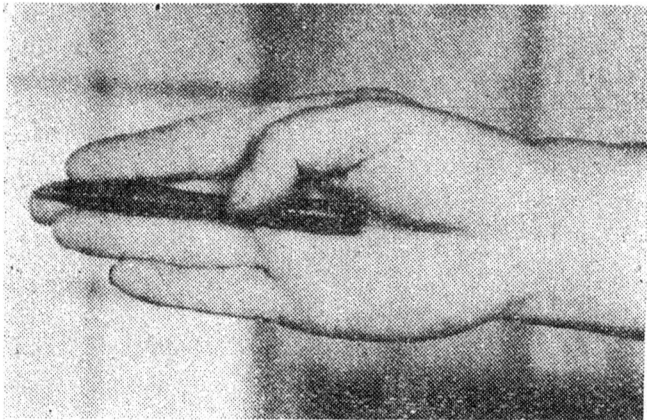

手裏剣の持ち方

Naruse demonstrating how to hold a Shuriken

打った瞬間

Technique 1
(right) Photograph 5 : One-handed Jodan Kame
(left) Naruse Sensei demonstrating the right hand's
position after release.

Advance on your opponent slowly and steadily. It is important to realize that your breathing at this point is very important. Remember the saying *Kage ni komoru*, stay in the shadows. Holding the Katana high over your head is a distinctive trait of this technique.

Focusing all your mental and physical power throw the Shuriken. Almost in the same beat rapidly shift into Haso stance. From this point the technique moves to Tohjutsu, sword art.

Technique 1
Photograph 6 : Katana positioning before sheathing #1

After you go into Haso Kamae, keeping your hands in the same grip, move the pommel of your sword just below Mizo-ochi, your solar plexus. Hold your sword straight out so it is parallel to the floor. At this point you should step back with your left foot, slightly on a diagonal, about 1 Shaku, 30 centimeters.

術の劍裏手

納刀の直前（二）

に高く構へる特異な構へ方である。

氣滿ちて、手裏劍を打ち終ると殆んど

一拍子に、す早く刀を八相に取つて構へ

る。

これからが卽ち刀術の領域だからであ

る。

八相に取つた刀は、兩手に持つたまゝ

柄頭をみぞおちの下につける位にして、

（右圖、納刀の直前、一）刀の切先を前方

に向けて水平に持つ。此の時、左足を一

尺程やゝ斜左後方に引くのである。次に

右手でずんと前方に刀を突き出して、

（上圖、納刀の直前、二）左手す早く鞘口

248

Technique 1
Photograph 7 : Katana positioning before sheathing #2

Next stab forward in a sharp motion with your right hand. This is shown in the Photograph titled *Katana positioning before sheathing #2.* Move your left hand quickly to the Saya-guchi and prepare to sheathe your sword.

剣裏手

二本目

納刀

を持ち、納刀の準備をする。

前方標的に注目しながら、しづかに納刀し終り、左足をもとへもどし、自然體に復して一本目を終るのである。

かうした動作は、手裏剣術を中心とした抜刀法であつて、自然、居合術の領域にもわたつてゐるものと見るべきである。

二本目は、刀を左手に持ち、垂直に前方にさし出して構へ乍ら打つのである。

243

Technique 1
Photograph 8 : Noh-toh – Sheathing Your sword

While keeping your eyes focused on the target ahead of you, quietly sheathe your sword. Your left hand grips the Say-guchi, your left foot returns to the initial position, and you stand naturally. This is the end of Technique 1.

These movements focus on Shuriken throwing techniques, however it is clearly a type of Batto, the art of sword drawing and cutting. Therefore it is quite natural to think of these techniques as a part of Iai Jutsu, or sword drawing.

二本目（前面）

二本目（側面）

この時、刀の鍔の右の
ふちを、敵の顔面、兩眼
の間につけて目標とする
のである。

三 本 目

三本目は、刀を左手に
持ち、左直向に切先を突
き出し乍ら打つのであ
る。

この時の刀の切先は、
敵の顔面、兩眼の間につ
けるのである。

244

82

二本目（前面）

二本目（側面）

Technique 2
Photographs showing Technique 2 from the front and side

For the second technique stand with your Katana in your left hand and throw while keeping the sword vertical. When throwing keep the right side of your Katana's Tsuba, sword guard, aimed at your opponent's face, right between his eyes. That is your target.

剣裏手

左圖四本目の二がそれである

五 本 目

　五本目は、刀を抜かず、柄を斜前方へ構へて打つ。（五本目の一）打ち終つた瞬間、す早く刀を抜いて、横に水平に持ち、（五本目の二）次いで前方へ向け、更に突

四 本 目

　四本目は、刀を左手に持ち、切先を前方に向けて下げながら打つのである。（四本目の一）或ひは柄頭を左に切先を右に向けて持つて打つ替手もある。

245

84

Technique 3
Photograph showing Technique 3

For the third technique stand with your Katana in your left hand with your arm straight out. The tip of your sword should be stabbing towards your enemy. Throw from this stance.

You should keep the tip of your sword pointed at the enemy's face, directly between his eyes.

手裏剣の術

四本目（二）　　　四本目（一）

き出して納刀する事前
の如くである。

以上五本の手のうち
に、「隠剣」（おんげん）
の手といふものが加へ
られる事もある。それ
は、一本のはじめに、
人知れず小形の手裏剣
を一本柄に隠し添へて
置き、一本打つた後、
續けうちにそれを柄か
ら取つて打つとか、或

246

86

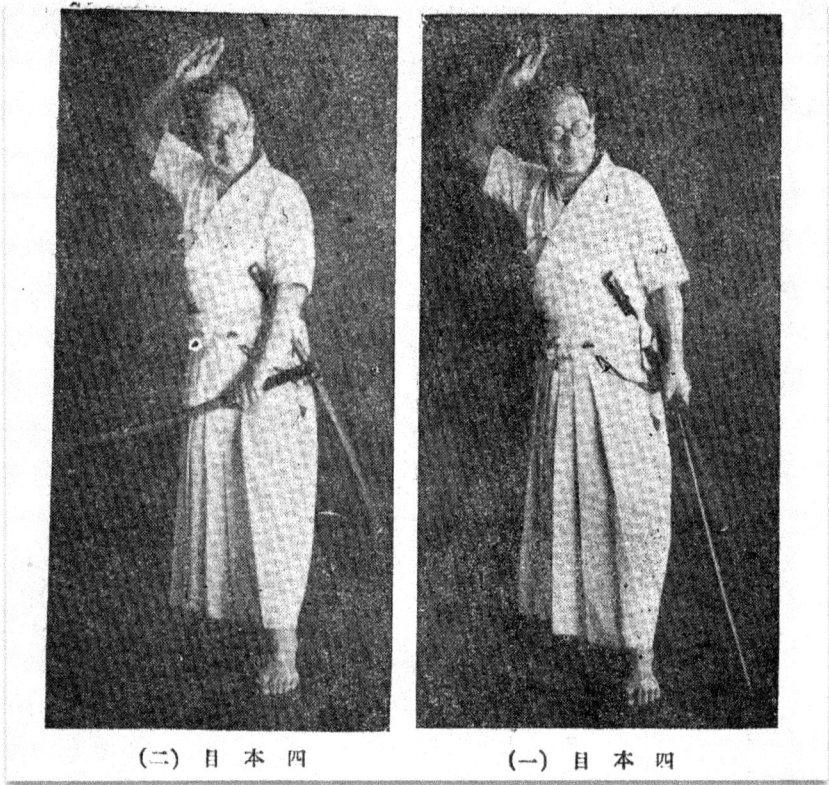

(二) 日 本 四　　　　　(一) 日 本 四

Technique 4
Right : Technique 4 Photograph 1
Left : Technique 4 Photograph 2

For the fourth technique, stand with the Katana in your left hand, with the tip of the sword pointing straight out in front. There are two ways to do this technique. In the first version, as you throw a Shuriken, allow the tip of your Katana to drop straight down. This is shown in Photograph 1.

The other way is to turn the tip of your Katana down and to the right as you throw a Shuriken. The pommel of your sword is facing your left side. This is shown in Photograph 2.

剣裏手

（二）目本五 　（一）目本五

ひは、鉢巻、又は袖の中、或ひは懷中などに祕めて置くとか、其の他二三の方法がある。

これ等は、單身多勢に對する時などに當意卽妙的に應用さるゝのであつて、從つて祕傳口傳も多いのである。

右のほか、坐打（さうち）、寢打（うち）、陰中（いんちう）（暗中のわざ）等の諸傳がある。

247

88

(二) 日 本 五　　　(一) 日 本 五

Technique 5
Right : Technique 5 Photograph 1
Left : Technique 5 Photograph 2

For the fifth technique you do not draw your Katana. Instead push the handle of your Katana diagonally forward and throw your Shuriken. This is shown in Photograph 1. As soon as you finish throwing the Shuriken, rapidly draw your Katana and hold it parallel to the ground. Then do a straight stab forward before sheathing your Katana. Photograph 2 shows the moment just before you sheathe your Katana.

Conclusion

This ends the introduction of these five techniques. I have included elements of Ongen, Secret Blade. For example in the first technique you are supposed to slip a small Shuriken into your palm without your opponent noticing it. Hold this blade against the handle of your Katana. After you throw your first Shuriken you can draw the one from against the handle of your Katana and throw again.

Another possibility is to conceal a Shuriken inside your Hachimaki, or headband, or in your Sode, or sleeve. Other places to conceal a Shuriken are in your breast pocket. There are two or three other methods as well. The reason for these precautions is to enable you to instantly react and utilize Shuriken whether against a single enemy or many. It goes without saying that there are a great many Kuden, orally transmitted teachings.

In addition to the techniques I have introduced here, there are also Za-uchi, Seated Throwing, Ne-uchi, Sleeping Throwing, Inchu, Throwing in the Dark and so on. There are many such techniques.

Naruse Kanji

Heidokyo
Mirror of the
Martial Way

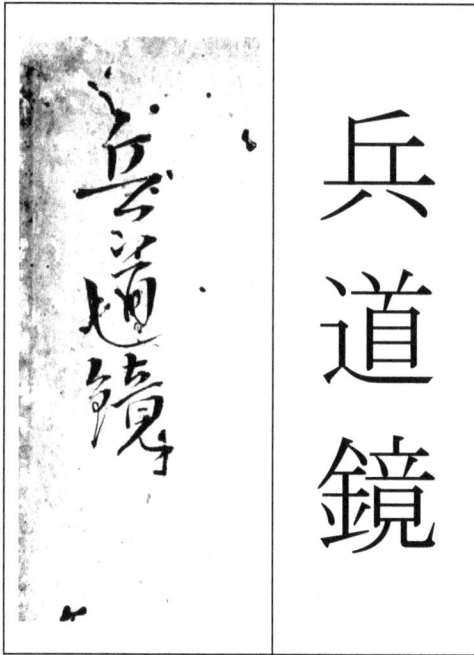

兵
道
鏡

Miyamoto Musashi

The Heidokyo, *Mirror of the Martial Way*, is an early work written by Miyamoto Musashi. The word "mirror" refers to something you should look at to see something, in this case the document "reflects" what a warrior should know. It was likely composed after Musashi's duels with the Yoshioka Clan in Kyoto. For many years it was thought to have been written by Miyamoto Musashi, however since a copy in Musashi's hand no longer exists, proof remained elusive.

However, the researcher Uozumi Takashi concluded that the document is by Musashi in his work *Musashi: A Man on the Path Japanese Should Walk* 2002. In his book Professor Uozumi was able to collect 6 versions of the Mirror of the Martial Way. These are all Shahon, meaning copies of the original. Each edition contains between 21 and 36 chapters, sometimes split over two volumes. Professor Uozumi describes them as follows:

	Edition	Chapters	Japanese Calendar	Western Calendar
1	Tada Family #1	28	Keicho 10	1605
2	Tada Family #2	28	Keicho 11	1606
3	Yamauchi Collection	30	Keicho 12	1607
4	Morita Family	36	Undated	
5	Makido Collection (Only volume 1)	21	Undated	
6	Imperial Library	22	Undated	

The Morita, Makido and Imperial Library editions do not contain the chapter on Shuriken, which is chapter 24 in the Tada Family editions and the 3rd entry in the second volume of the Yaumachi Collection document. This next section will translate two versions of this passage, one from the Yamauchi Collection and the other from Tada Family #1, which differ somewhat.

Handwritten Section from the Yamauchi Collection Dated 1607

Transcript of the Yamauchi Collection Dated 1607

手離剣打様之事

手離剣打やうハ人指ゆひを脇指の〇に置て手をはやく先
へつきはなす心なるへし。手くひすくミかたしなやかな
るよき也。目付のほしをこふしにて打やうにすへき也。
間積の事敵合一間の時ハ太刀先五寸上て打へし。
二間八一尺六五立て打へき也。初ハほしより高き心に
切先あかりに立膝に少よわく打習へき也。勢力出る時
たたまりてほしよりつかり切先もさかる物也。
猶口傳多シ。

English Translation of
Mirror of the Martial Way
Yamauchi Collection Dated 1607

On the Topic of How to Throw Shuriken

Shuriken Uchi, throwing a sword as a Shuriken, should be done with your index finger on the back of the Wakizashi short sword. You should focus on throwing rapidly straight in front of you, so it sticks in your target. Keep your wrist rigid but your shoulder should be relaxed. Fix your eye on your target and throw as if trying to strike it with your fist.

When judging the distance to your target, if the distance is 1 Ken, 1.8 meters, aim your sword to strike 5 Sun, 15 centimeters, above your target. If the distance is 2 Ken, 3.6 meters, aim to strike 1 Shaku and 5 ~ 6 Sun, 45 ~ 46 cm above your target.

Initially, you should throw to strike higher than the spot you aim for. You should keep your knees loose when training.

When you throw with power you will hit lower on your target and the tip of your sword will dip down. Be aware that there are many Kuden, orally transmitted teachings.

Transcript of the Tada Family Edition Dated 1606

手裏剣打様之事

手裏剣の打様は、人さしを、刀のみねにおきて、敵をきる様に打べし。打たんと思ふゆへに、たたざる也。手くびすくませて、かたをしなやかに、目付所のほしを、こぶしにてつく様にすべし。はじめには、ちかくやはらかに、切先あがりに立様にすべし。間を積事、敵合一間の時には、五寸、太刀先を上て打べし。一間半の時は、一尺立、二間の時は一尺五寸立打べし。ほしより高く立事はくるしからず。下がる事あしく、勢力入る程、ほしよりさがり、切先うつぶきて、あたる物也。きをはる事あしく、うつ時の身の懸、あをのきてむねを出し、足を出し、うしろえのる事、いかほどものる程よし。いきは、ゑいゑいとそらうち一つ二つして、のり上る時、引いき長くして、はなるる時、とつと云ういきにて、はなすべし。ゑいと打咄すいき、あしく、工夫肝要也。

English Translation of:
Mirror of the Martial Way
Tada Family Edition Dated 1606

On the Topic of How to Throw Shuriken

To throw your sword as a Shuriken place your Hitosashi Yubi, index finger, on the back of the blade and throw as if you are trying to cut your enemy. If you think of this strike as a hit, it will miss. Keep your wrist rigid but your shoulder relaxed. Fix your eyes on your target and throw as if punching at it with your fist.

Initially, you should throw gently from a close distance. Raise the point of your blade so it is vertical. As you increase the distance you should make adjustments. If an enemy is 1 Ken, 1.8 meters, away then aim the end of your blade at a spot 5 Sun, 15 centimeters, above your target. If 1.5 Ken, 2.7 meters away, then raise it another 1 Shaku, 30 centimeters. If 2 Ken, 3.6 meters, away then aim the tip of your blade 1.5 Shaku, 45 centimeters, above your target.

It is not a problem if your blade strikes higher than the point you were aiming at, however if it strikes lower that is bad. Putting too much power in your throw will result not only in the blade striking below your target but the tip will be stuck in facing down with the handle up.

It is bad to tense your whole body up when throwing. Your body should hang naturally, facing forward with your chest out. Step out with your [left] foot and put your weight on your back foot. You can put as much weight on your back leg as you want.

Breathe out an *Ei! Ei!* sound once or twice without throwing. When throwing take in a deep breath and throw while expelling a *Totsu!* Sound. It is bad to throw with an exhalation of *Ei!* You should work on developing ways to make this work for you.

Chishin School
An Illustrated Guide to
Shuriken
Excerpt 1:
Chishin School Densho

図解 手裏剣術 藤田西湖著

By Fujita Seiko
1964

Translator's introduction

Fujita Seiko (1898 ~ 1966)

An Illustrated Guide to Shuriken
Excerpt 1: Chisin School Densho
By Fujita Seiko
1964

This section is a translation of the schools of Shuriken throwing that relate to Miyamoto Musashi. This book is by Fujita Seiko (1898 ~ 1966) who was a martial arts researcher and the 14th and final head of the Koga Ryu School of Ninjutsu. Fujita records the Mokuroku, catalogue of techniques, sections of Densho, instructive documents, gives dimensions for Shuriken and illustrates Shuriken throwing techniques.

Fujita Seiko copied the Densho and illustrations for his book. It seems likely that he read Naruse's book and followed up on some of the leads to find more information regarding Chishin School Shuriken.

Chishin Ryu Shuriken Mokuroku
Chishin School: A Catalogue of Shuriken Lessons and Techniques

知新流手裏剣目録

一 手裏剣離之事
一 手裏剣軽重之事
一 同長短之事
一 同手之内之事
一 同足踏之事
一 打出目付之事
一 指屈伸之事
一 上下打之事
右八ケ条立打也

一 居打之事
一 左右打之事
一 二本打之事
一 三本打之事
一 四本打之事
一 三間打之事
一 手裏剣留打様
右八ケ条也

一 風切
一 腰刀
一 懐剣
一 夜打様
右三ケ条者免許之伝也

目録如件
右之条々令相伝畢猶於鍛錬修行有
之者免許之伝口打可令相伝者也仍

大和郡山之住士
　飯嶋市兵衛
同
　飯嶋源太左衛門
同
　日置金左衛門
尾州之浪士
　浅野伝右衛門
同国之住士
　丹羽織江

Chishin Ryu Shuriken Mokuroku
Chishin School:
A Catalogue of Shuriken Lessons and Techniques

- How to Release the Shuriken
- The Proper Range of Weight for Shuriken
- The Proper Range of Length for Shuriken
- The Proper Way to Step When Throwing Shuriken
- Where to Look When Throwing
- How to Apply Proper Pressure With Your Fingers
- How to Strike Targets Above and Below You

The above 8 topics deal with throwing while standing

- Throwing While Seated
- How to Throw Left or Right
- Throwing Two Shuriken
- Throwing Three Shuriken
- Throwing Four Shuriken
- Striking a Target Three Intervals Away
- How to Throw Shuriken at a Target
- Cutting the Wind

These are 8 topics

- Throwing at Night
- Kaiken (A small knife in a scabbard kept inside the shirt.)
- Koshi-gatana ("Waist Katana" another word for Katana.)

The above three topics are taught to those who receive Menkyo, full transmission.

The certificate establishes that you received full transmission of all teachings of this school and have trained diligently. Granting of this certificate means that you may pass on these teachings as long as the person you instruct is an appropriate student.

Order of Succession:

Founder of the Chishin School
A Samurai of Yamatokori (In Nara Prefecture)
Ishima Ichihyoe
↓
A Samurai of Yamatokori
Ishima Genta Saemon
↓
A Samurai of Yamatokori
Heki Kinsaemon
↓
A Ronin of Oshu
Asano Denuemon
↓
A Samurai of Oshu
Tanba Orie

Granted on an auspicious day in August the 6th year of Horeki
1756

Chishin Ryu Shuriken Menkyo
Chishin School of Shuriken : License of Transmission

知新流手裏剣免許

当流手裏剣者知新流剣術之内抜出一流独心不浅多年出精稽古之仮神妙之至候依

之夜之打形並懐剣腰刀打形不残令伝授候猶此上無怠慢工夫鍛錬可為専一候向後

独心之蟄於有之者戯事心得不申様以固可有之指南候仍而免許如件

Chishin Ryu Shuriken Menkyo
Chishin School of Shuriken : License of Transmission

This school of Shuriken is descended from and received its teachings through the Chishin School. It is the product of many years of dedicated training, without interruption until bearer of this certificated achieved enlightenment to the inner mysteries of this school. Thus you have been taught every aspect of:
Throwing at Night
Throwing the Kaiken and Koshigatana
It is expected you will devote yourself entirely to forging your skill diligently and develop your own Kufu, or knacks and small improvements.

You have been granted full authority to pass on these teachings and grant licenses however you must be sure of the character of those you teach. If you judge them to be deceptive in character you should not instruct them. These are the conditions of this license.

印可伝授書

知新流手裏劍と云ふは強きに限らず弱きを厭はず兎に角早く打ち出し當るを専一とする也　先の柄に手を掛ると見たら直ちに打ち出すなり　目録の内に打出し目付と有るは是也　手裏劍を初めて教ゆるに先つ手前の右足を先の目當て先きえ向けて踏み打つなり　打出す劍と足と一所に打出す事也足踏み専一也足踏みそまつに心得ては夜の打様に不當　桃燈又は行燈杯有之場所にて打つ時は光をおゝて打つ事也　拔劍を強くきかせんと思はゝ劍を柔かに持つて振り打ちに打たは劍當りきくなり　拔又打劍の右より立つは離れに指先のきく故に打たは劍當りきくなり　拔又打劍の右より立つは手のひらにて打つ故に押しつけ離れる故なり　劍の上より立つは離れをおしむ故也　手離れをおしまぬ様に心得打つ事専一なり笠かむり打つには間近き場所にて打つ心得よろし　手裏劍留に打ち通すもよろし水にぬれたる劍は随分やわかに持ち打つなり　又　幼年の者に大劍を打たするには肩えかけて打たする事　長き物を打つには中程のつり合を考え打つ事なり

Chishin Ryu Inka Denjusho
Chishin School:
Certificate of Transmission and Authorization to Teach

The philosophy of Chishin School Shuriken is not about throwing hard or soft, rather to throw quickly and strike your target accurately. As soon as you opponent places his hand on the handle of his Katana, you should throw. This is what is written in the *Where to Look When Throwing* chapter of the *Catalogue of Techniques of the Chishin School.*

The first lesson in our school of Shuriken is to use your right foot to aim at your opponent. Step forward with your right foot and throw the moment it contacts the ground. You should focus your training on throwing the moment your foot contacts the ground. If you are careless about how you step you will be unable to hit targets at night.

At night, when throwing a Shuriken at a person holding a paper lantern, block the source of light and throw.

If you want the blade to strike hard, hold the Shuriken lightly as you raise your hand and throw. This will cause your blade to strike hard.

If the end of your Shuriken is leaning to the right, the way your fingertips apply pressure when throwing is the problem. If the end of your Shuriken is leaning to the left, the way you apply pressure with your palm when throwing is the problem. If the end of the Shuriken is pointed up, you are releasing the Shuriken too late. You should devote yourself to finding the ideal way to release the Shuriken.

When throwing at a person wearing a straw hat remember you will need to be closer than you think. This also applies to throwing Shuriken at a target board.

Hold Shuriken that are wet as lightly as possible when throwing.

When teaching young people how to throw Daiken (the largest Shuriken?) focus only on throwing with one arm.

When throwing a Shuriken at something long, pick you target somewhere in the middle.

目録の内に四本打といふ有り　四本の劔を紙にて狀を封ずる様に巻き劔はうち
違いに包み其儘打ては二本の劔はたしかに立つ事なり　又はひとえの袋に入れ
て打つ事なり　袱紗などに包み結ぶは悪るし　結び目のあらば打ちがたし　能
くく心得べし

劔がしらの下り立つは押付のきく故也　横平に當るは大指のすべる故也　又り
きみの有る故もあり　是れは能く見合せ直す事なり

懐劍手の内は両様におしえてよろし引上げの手の下らぬ様におしえる事也
懐劍長さは六寸より九寸五分迄　扨小劍にて板金を通すは劔のきく事を見るに
あらず手離れすなをに離るゝ事を見る為なり　劔のひずみて立つものは心能く
ぬけざる事なり　懐劍のさやを下え抜き打つ事なり

扨　手裏劍修行の人の心得と申すは常々客に参り候はゞ　先づ茶を出し候はゞ
茶碗を右の膝元に置く事　煙草盆を出し候はゞ随分と手近かに引付け置く事な

三七

In the Mokuroku catalogue scroll there is a technique called Yon-hon Uchi, throwing four Shuriken at the same time. Wrap four Shuriken up inside a piece of paper. Since two of the four Shuriken are facing the opposite direction when you wrap them up, at least two points will strike. You can also place them inside a bag and throw.

Wrapping them up with a Fukusa, a small silk cloth commonly used for cleaning tea ceremony implements, is not a good idea. The knot you tie will adversely affect your throw.

If the Shuriken is hanging down after you throw, then you have applied too much pressure. If the Shuriken is leaning either to the left or right after striking the target, it is because your thumb is slipping when you throw. When you see these kinds of errors, you should immediately correct your technique.

Our school teaches that the Kaiken, knife kept in the breast pocket, is handled the same way as a Shuriken, you shouldn't allow the hand you raise to throw to drop too low. A Kaiken should be between 6 ~ 9.5 Sun, 18 ~ 29 centimeters, long.[9]

You may have heard of throwing a Ko-ken, small sword, through a sheet of metal. However, it is not about throwing a blade adeptly, instead it is about making it appear as if you have thrown a blade when you have not.

If a blade bends when it strikes, it means you have completely lost your focus. This school teaches to pull the scabbard down off your Kaiken before you throw.

On another note I would like to give some advice to those going on Shuriken Shugyo, travelling around and learning from different schools. Please behave like a normal guest. If they offer you tea when you arrive, place the teacup beside your right knee. If an ashtray is offered, be sure to pull it very close to you. While all the above applies to Shuriken, it also applies to Sansu, the Japanese folding fan.

---

[9] Kaiken or "Breast Pocket Knife" was a common weapon carried by travelers. Carrying swords was illegal in the Edo Era unless you were a Samurai, however small knives were allowed. That being said the definition of "small" became rather elastic and travelers began carrying rather large "pocketknives."

り　手裏剣に限らず扇子にても右の心得よろし

飛龍劔　腰刀は抜き放し下えさげむねを平手にて持ちそえ　つる〳〵と足をは
こび間合を見て打ち離す事也　打ちかゝるに振り上げ打ち出す節しばらく刀を
引き出して離すことなり　打ちかゝる離れの節柄を下え引き下げ離すことなり
腰刀長さ一尺二三寸より七八寸よろし　長き腰刀は不好　目当は土俵にて打
たする事なれ共　近年は目当板にて打たする事になりたり　然し飛び返えり候
えばあやまち有る事故用心すべし

扨　門人にて無之人手裏劔所望之者有之候はゝ　初め五本随分やわらかに打ち
て見せる事なり　次に五本は常々稽古之通りに打ち見せ　三度目に板金を打つ
心にて打つ事也　三度之外打つ事なかれ　他人に打ち見せるには居打立打二本
打つ事　懐劔は二三本打ち見せる也　何れも沢山に打つ事なかれ　小劔は四品
の外かたく打つべからず

Hiryuken, Flying Dragon Sword. Draw your Koshi-gatana and hold it pointed down with your left hand on the handle and the palm of your right hand on the back of the sword. Press in on your enemy with smooth footsteps and then throw your sword like a Shuriken. When you are ready to throw bring the sword up into Jodan Kamae and, the moment you release, pull down on the handle. The best length for a Koshi-gatana is from 1 Shaku and 2 or 3 Sun to 7 or 8 Sun, 36 ~ 39 centimeters or 51 ~ 54 centimeters. Long Koshi Gatana are not good.

Note:

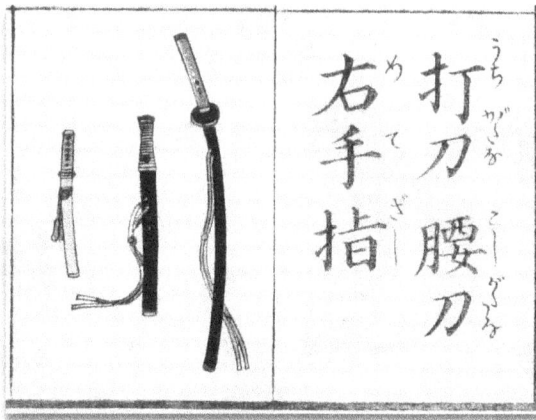

Two Hundred Illustrations of Weapons 武器皕圖
by Kobayashi Yuken 1848

Uchi Gatana (Katana)
Koshi Gatana (Katana)
Medezashi (Utility knife /Shuriken)

Samurai practicing Shuriken from *Illustrations of Learning* 写真学筆 by Maki Bokusen 牧墨僊 (1775－1824). The man on the bottom left is holding a Metezashi.

When a member of this school is demonstrating Shuriken throwing to a person not in the school, first throw five Shuriken in a gentle manner. Next, throw another set of five Shuriken as you normally would during training. For the final set throw with power as if you are trying to pierce a metal plate. Do not throw more than three sets.

When showing others throw two times from a seated position and two times from a standing position. When demonstrating throwing the Kaiken, knife kept in the breast of the shirt, only throw two or three times. It is not necessary to demonstrate more than that. Never show anything more than the four basic throws with the small blades.

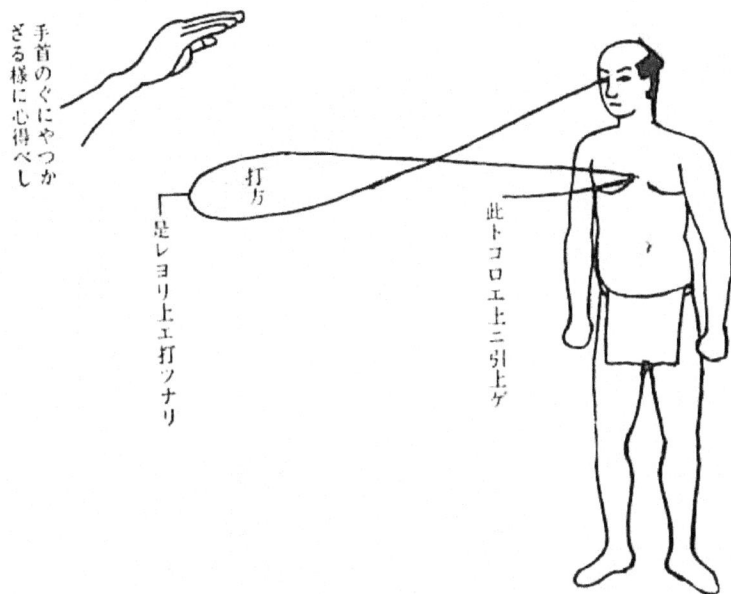

擬　劔を拵うるには　小劔は重さ二十五匁より三十五匁迄　長さ五寸より四五

分迄二三分通用なり夫れも人々物好み次第なり

此トコロエ上ニ引上ゲ

打方

是レヨリ上エ打ツナリ

手首のくにやつか

ざる様に心得べし

It is important to not allow your wrist to bend.

Direction of throw

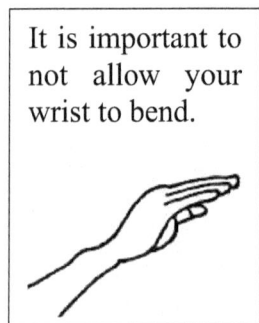

You should throw before this point.

Raise above this point.

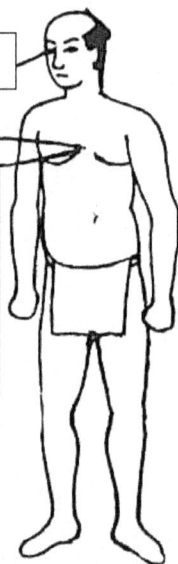

打万

擬劍を拆うるには　小劍は重さ二十五匁より三十五匁迄　長さ五寸より四五

分迄二三分通用なり夫れも人々物好み次第なり

If you are going to make Shuriken, small blades should be between 25 Monme and a maximum of 35 Monme, 94 ~ 131.25 grams. The length should be between 5 Sun and 4 or 5 Bun, 16 ~ 16.5 centimeters. The weight of most Shuriken is within 2 or 3 Bun, 0.6 ~ 0.9 centimeters, so it really is up to each person to decide.

Translator's Note:
The old measurement varied considerably over time according to location. I have used these measurements:
One 寸 Sun is 3.03 centimeters.
One Bun is .3 centimeters
One Monme is 3.75 grams
Illustration of the measurements:

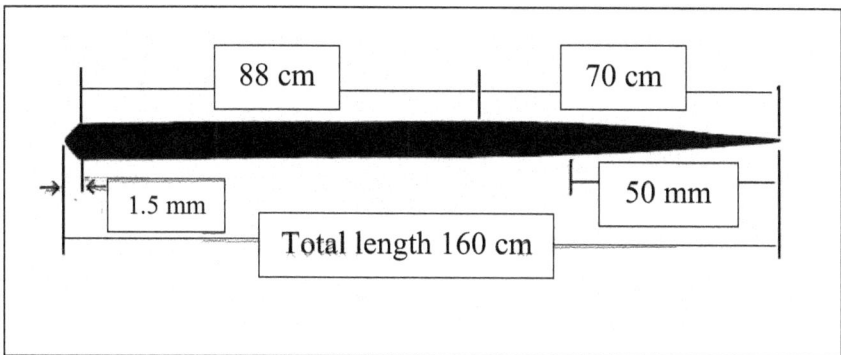

足先を向の足先えむけて引上る手と一所に足を踏込み打つ也　打ちかくる手と

一所に踏込む事也

初め人に教ゆるに　五六尺の間合にて随分やわらかに打ちおしゅる事なり　追

々剣の立つに付いて　足首丈つゝしさり　次第〱にしされば本間えなる事

なり

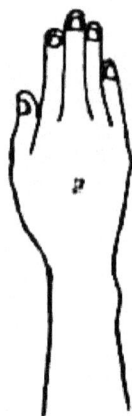

此の通り指の
直なる様に

Point the end of your foot at the tip of the opponent's foot. Raise your arm as you step and release as your foot contacts the ground. Throw the Shuriken and plant your foot at the same time.

The distance for beginners should be around 5 or 6 Shaku, 150 ~ 180 centimeters. Teach them how to throw gently. Later after they become able to stick Shuriken in the target increase the distance little by little, one foot-width at a time.

Your fingers should be kept straight like this.

稽古の節劔を取り落す事有り　直ちに拾ろいて打つ事悪し　落した劔にかまわ
ず手に有る劔を打ち切りしあとにて拾い打つ事なり　劔を手の内え能くなつけ
る様に指をつたい様に打つ事専一なり
劔を打つに我が手のひらの先え見ゆる様に心得打つ也　打ち出す時劔より足の
先え出る事悪るし　劔と足と一所に踏込む事なり
大指の離れぬ様に心得打つ事也　大指すべれば劔横ひらに當るなり　又劔の離
れをおしめばたてに立つなり　懐劔初めて教ゆるに手の内は定法なり　目付は
鼻より下を心がけ打つなり

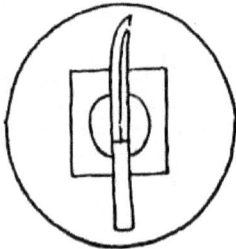

此の通りに当る様に不
立様に打たせる事也ケ
様教えれば則ち立なり
足れ秘伝なり

When training you may accidentally drop a Shuriken on the ground. However it is bad form to immediately pick it up and throw it. Don't concern yourself with the Shuriken you dropped and instead throw the ones remaining. After finishing that pick up the one you dropped and throw it. It is important for you to learn how to handle the Shuriken. You need to focus completely on training your fingers develop a sense of how to hold the Shuriken so you can throw them comfortably.

Concentrate on looking past the ends of your finger when you throw Shuriken. When throwing, allowing your foot to move before your blade is a bad habit. The blade and your foot should move in unison.

Be sure to not allow your thumb to lose contact as you throw. If your thumb slips it will cause the blade to stick in the target leaning to one side or the other.

If you release the Shuriken too late it will stick in the target vertically.

There is a standard way to introduce how to handle and throw the Kaiken. You should focus on throwing at a point below the nose.

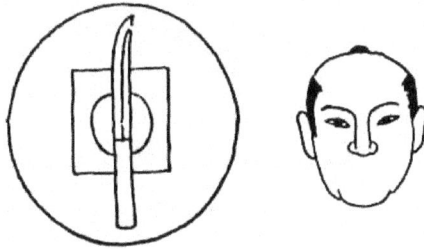

此の通りに当たる様に不立様に打たせる事也ケ様教えれば則ち立なり是秘伝なり

This diagram illustrates how you should throw and how not to throw. If taught according to these principles you will immediately be able to throw accurately. This is a secret teaching.

四〇

懐劔と腰刀は離れのおしみて放つ心也

懐劔之目付は鼻より下を打つ心也　懐劔は胸より下らぬ様に打つなり

劔に十分一之劔というは八十目の劔一本に八匁の劔二本是れを八匁劔を打つ

次に八十目の劔を打ち　又八匁の劔を打つケ様に入違いに打たゞれは大劔にて

も小劔にても打ち覚える為なり

丸き物を打つには指三本かけて打つ也左之通り

When throwing Kaiken or Koshi Gatana you should hold on to the handle a bit longer before releasing. When releasing the Kaiken you should focus your aim at a point below the nose. However you should be careful never allow the Kaiken to strike below the chest.

"One in Ten Shuriken" refers to throwing 1 or 2 Shuriken weighing 8 Monme, or 30 grams, for every 8 ~ 10 regular Shuriken. After throwing 1 or 2 of the 8 Monme Shuriken, throw 8 ~10 regular Shuriken and then mix in the 8 Monme Shuriken. By switching the weights around you can get used to throwing both Daiken, long Shuriken, and Shoken, small Shuriken.

When throwing objects with round handles you should hold and throw with three fingers. This is shown in the illustration below.

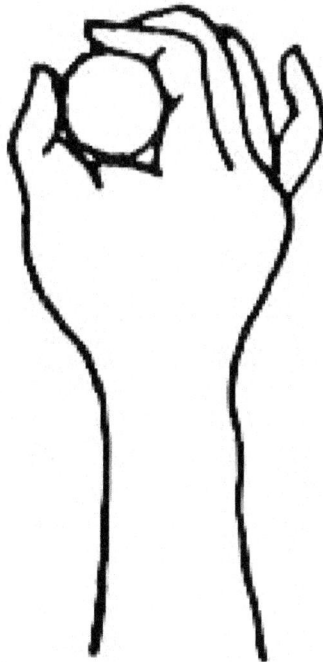

居打は打出す節いしきを少し上げて度々に打つ事也

手裏劔當は先の左より返しこみ打つ事也　常々稽古に足踏み第一也　初めに教

ゆる節足は目當の通りえ右足を踏み振り上げ打ちかゝる時足を一所に踏み出す

足の踏み出す串劔より早く出るは悪し

上下左右之乱劔の者えは目當を見はる事悪し　劔取る節手本を見て振り上げる

と一諸に目當てを見て打っか　又は手前の足先を見て振上げる迄目當を見る事

悪し

When throwing from a seated position, focus your aim slightly higher than your actual target. Practice this repeatedly.

Shuriken-tome, Shuriken Stop, is when you throw across your left side.

The most important lesson to train repeatedly is how to step. This should be the first thing you teach beginners. Your right foot should be aimed at your target. Then, step forward as your arm begins to rise. Your throw and your foot contacting the ground should be simultaneous. If your foot lands before you throw, you are doing it wrong.

People that end up with wild throws, as in the Shuriken stuck in the target facing upward, hanging downward, leaning left or right, are doing a bad job of picking their target. Such a person may be looking at their hands when drawing the Shuriken and then focusing on the target as they raise their arm. Another possibility is they are focusing on the leading foot as they raise their arm to throw. This is a poor way to aim your throw.

常々足踏みは左の通りなり

打出す時此処え
踏み出すなり

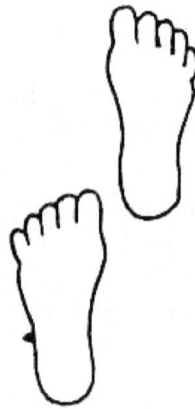

○

右の通り足踏みは左足の大指の頭通りえ　右足のきびすを踏出す時右足を二ッ
丈踏み出す也　又右足を踏み付けて打つもよろし　左足はきびすを踏付けぬ様
に心得専一也　万事足は軽く踏む事なり
遠間はさかに劔を取り打ち出す時指先にて少し押える様にあしらいて離す事な

You should study the illustration below carefully, it shows how to plant your feet.

This is how you should be stepping when you throw.

踏み出すなり　打出す時此処え　○

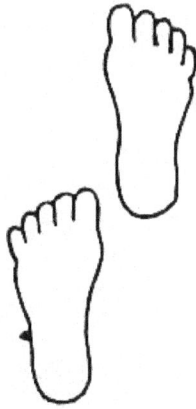

As you step, your right foot should pass over the big toe of your left foot. When stepping, your right heel should travel about two foot spans. As I said before you should throw as your right foot contacts the ground. Another important point is not allowing the heel of your left foot to be planted on the ground, keep it off the ground. Always be sure to step lightly when moving.

When throwing a long distance you will be holding the Shuriken reversed in your hand. As you release, press with the fingertips.

り

稽古五本劔を左の腰通りえ下げ　一本づゝ取り打つ事也　腰通りと云うは劔打

懸り直ちに刀の柄に手のかかり申す為めに持ち覚ゆるためなり　五本劔は劔と

心得ず　一本打出し直ちに柄に手をかけ申す心なり　刀の鯉口を持つ心なり

当り左右え乱劔を直す事　巾二三分長さ目当板の丈に白紙をたち板えたて張り

打すれば左右はづれ直る事なり

甘シヤウ劔と云う有リ　足は一子相伝同様の事なれば印可つかはし候とゝ此カ

ンシヤウ劔は伝授無用也

目当四寸に五寸と定むる事は元祖飯嶋氏竹村与右衛え打見せ候節　目当は何程

に致し稽古致し候やと尋ね候時四五寸の目当と申すに付き四寸に五寸と定むる

なり

126

When training, keep five Shuriken in your waist on the left side. Draw them one at a time and throw. The reason to keep Shuriken in your waist on the left side and practice throwing them is to train your left hand to move to the handle of your Katana. Though you have five Shuriken in your waist, the point is to train your hand to immediately grab the handle of your sword after each throw. Your hand should grab the Koi-guchi, the top of the scabbard.

The next topic is how to correct wild throws that lean to the left or right. Prepare a piece of white paper 2 or 3 Bun, 6 ~ 9 millimeters, wide and as long as a Shuriken target board. Throwing at this will correct the problem of Shuriken leaning to the right or left after striking the target.

Within the teachings of the Chishin School there is a technique called Ama Sho Ken (meaning unknown.) This teaching is only passed on to a single student and thus is not part of this certification and will not be taught to you.

The founder of this school, Ijima Sensei, who was a student of Takemura Youemon, once asked him, "What are the proper dimensions for a Shuriken target?" In response Takemura answered, "I would say 4 or 5 Sun, 12 ~15 centimeters, is best." Therefore we have decided to use targets with 12 and 15 centimeter marks.

You are receiving this certification scroll authenticating that you have learned the inner mysteries of this art. Your dedication to training has exceeded that of others and you never were lax in your Shugyo, intense learning. You are now authorized to teach the Chishin School Shuriken arts to students, however if you sense a person is not of good character, absolutely do not teach them. That is a condition of this certification.

此印可之一巻者手裏剣伝授之蘊奥也然処貴殿之執心他勝殊修行不怠故授与之畢
後門人に伝えむとあらば必ず其人の器量を計りて可伝妄りに不可伝仍而奥書
如件

大和郡山之住士
流祖　飯嶋市兵衛
同　飯嶋源太左衛門
同　日置金左衛門
尾州之浪士
浅野伝右衛門
同国之住士
丹羽織江

Chishin School
Shuriken
Throwing
Excerpt 2: Training

図解 手裏剣術 藤田西湖 著

An Illustrated Guide
By Fujita Seiko
1964

直打法による剣

手から打ち離された剣を、とばこうに行く。

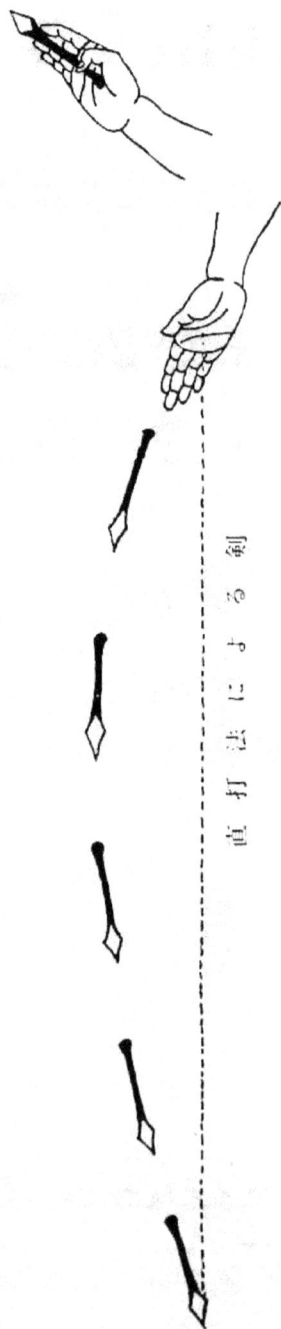

Shuriken Throwing

This is called Choku-uchi, a method for throwing a Shuriken straight into a target without spinning. When released from the hand, the Shuriken should fly on this trajectory.

刀法供用手裏剣術 *Toho Kyoyo Shuriken Jutsu*
Using the Katana With Shuriken
知新流 *Chishin Ryu*
Chishin School

手裏剣を右手に隠し持って敵と相対し、

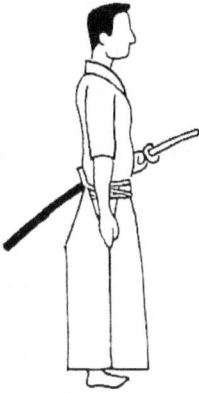

敵、刀の柄に手を掛けると見るや、右足を敵の目を目当てに踏み出すとともに手裏剣を打ち、手は直ちに柄にかけ、

Chishin School Fundamental

Conceal the Shuriken in your right hand as you face the enemy.

As soon as you see your enemy move his hand to the Tsuka, or handle, of his sword, step forward with your right foot. Throw the Shuriken, aiming for his eyes, then immediately grab the Tsuka of your own Katana.

敵がひるむところ
を

踏み込んで切る。

Chishin School Fundamental

As your enemy is reacting to your strike…

…step in and cut.

立礼して後、

一本目

手裏剣五本を右前
半に差し、日本刀
を右手に提げて出
る。

Chishin School Technique 1

1	2
Start with five straight Shuriken tucked into the front of your Obi. Your Nihonto, Katana, is in your right hand as you step forward and stop.	Do a Tachi-rei, or standing bow, then…

まず左手で鞘口を
持ち、鍔五分ばか
り離して刀の柄を
握り、右足を斜め
前方に踏み出し、

刀を左手に持ちか
えて帯刀する。

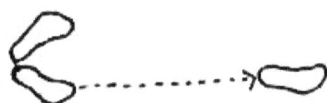

Chishin School Technique 1	
3	**4**
Slide your Katana into your Obi and hold onto the scabbard with your left hand.	Your first move is to open the Koiguchi. This means to push on the Tsuba, sword guard, with your left thumb, open 1.5 centimeters, unsticking the sword from it's scabbard. Grip the Tsuka with your right hand and step diagonally forward with your right foot.

刀を抜き、片手八

相に構え、

右足をもどし、柄
と右手腕とを併行
させ、右胸脇に構
え、左手で鞘口を
握ったまま直立し
て前方標的に見入
る。

Chishin School Technique 1	
5	**6**
Draw your Katana and hold it in your right hand in Hasso Kamae, with the blade vertical. Then step back with your right foot to your starting stance.	As you step back, ensure the handle of your sword as well as your right hand and arm all move in unison with your body. Stay in this Migi Waki Gamae, or Stance With the Sword by Your Right Side. Keeping your left hand on the Koiguchi, stand straight and stare directly at the person who is your target.

持ち終ったら、手を下げ、標的に向かって数歩進む。

次に刀を左手に持ちかえて構え、前方を凝視しつつ、右手で手裏剣を一本抜き出し右手に持つ。

Chishin School Technique 1	
7	**8**
As you stare intensely at the enemy in front of you, switch the Katana to your left hand. With your right hand remove one Shuriken from your belt and hold it in your right hand.	After you have positioned the Shuriken in your hand allow your arm to hang down. Take several steps towards your target.

左上段に構えた刀
をさらに高く構え、
手裏剣を打つと、
直ちに、

間合をはかって気
合とともに左手に
持った刀を
左片手上段
に構え、手
裏剣を打ち
構えにして、左半
身になってじりじ
りと敵にせまる。

Chishin School Technique 1

9	10
Focus all your energy as you judge the distance to your target. Bring your left hand holding the Katana up to Kata-te Jodan, One-handed upper stance and, at the same time, ready your right hand to throw the Shuriken. Keep your left side forward as you slowly and steadily advance on your target.	Continue to raise your Katana to a higher Jodan Kamae and throw your Shuriken. Then immediately…

刀を八相に構える。

Chishin School Technique 1

11

...go into Haso Kamae, with the Katana by your side.

次に刀の切先を前
方に向け、左足を
斜め左後方に引き
右手の刀は前方に
突き出し、左手は
すばやく鞘いを握
り、納刀の姿勢に

Chishin School Technique 1

12

Next, point the end of your Katana forward and pull your left foot diagonally backwards. Hold the Katana in your right hand and push your arm forward. Your left hand should go to the Koiguchi, carp's mouth, of your scabbard in a quick motion. Begin sheathing your sword.

左手は刀の鞘口を
握り、左足をもど
し、もとの自然体
となり、一本目終
る。

しずかに納刀。

Chishin School Technique 1	
13	**14**
Quietly sheathe your Katana.	With your left hand still on the Koi-guchi, move your left foot beside your right and return to your natural standing position.
Note: The following page shows the entire sequence	

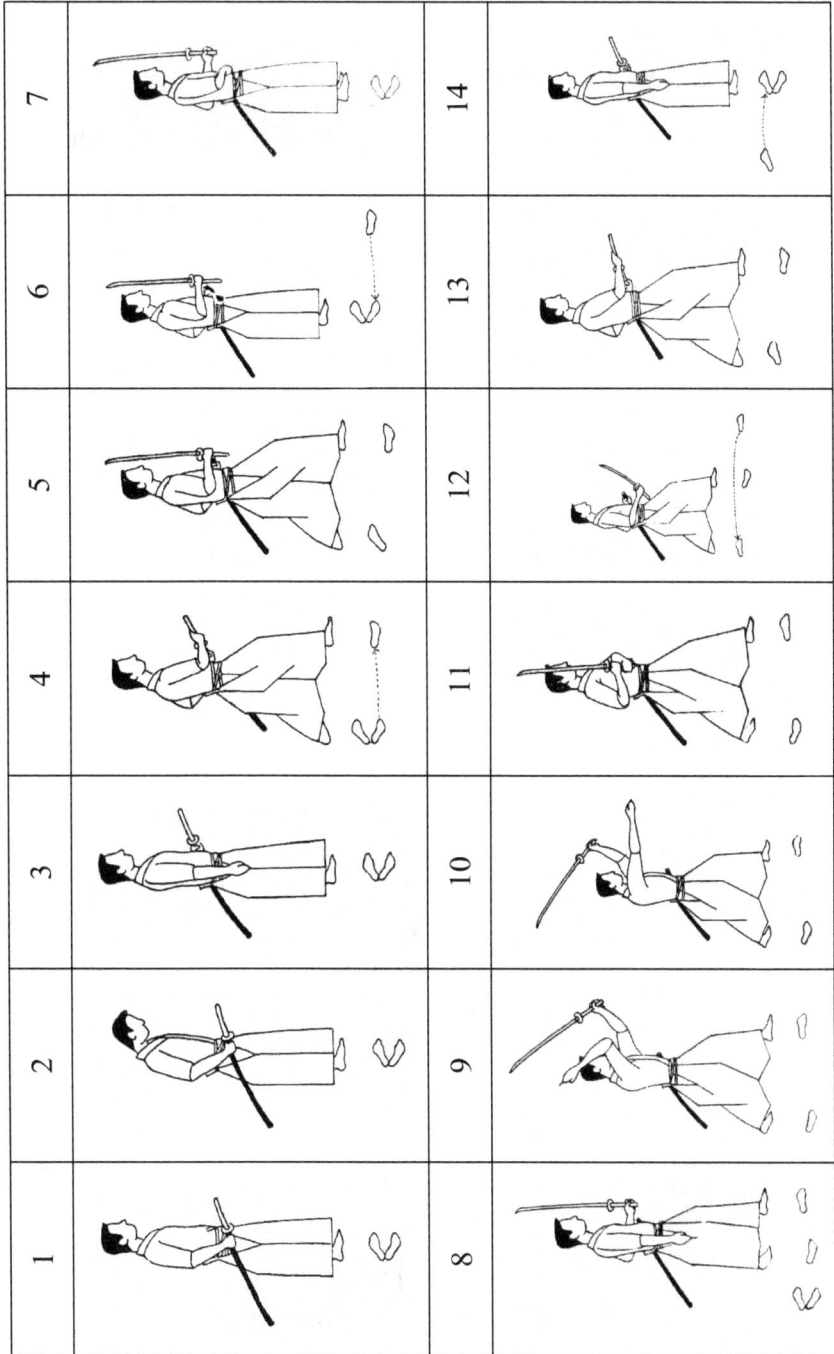

Chishin School Technique 2

Hold your Katana straight up in front of you with your left hand. From that stance throw your Shuriken. Use the Tsuba, sword guard, to guide your throw. Keep the edge of the Tsuba on his face and aim to throw between his eyes.

二本目

左手に持った刀を
垂直に前にさし出
して構えながら打
つ。このとき、刀
の鍔のふちを敵の
顔面、両眼の間に
つけて目標とする。

Chishin School Technique 3

Holding the Katana in your left hand with your arm extended, straight out, throw your Shuriken. The tip of your sword is forward. When doing this technique keep the tip of the sword on the enemy's face, directly between his eyes.

三本目

刀を左手に持ち、左直向に切先を突き出しながら打つ。このとき刀の切先は、敵の顔、両眼の間につける。

同じく四本目の替手・

柄頭を左に切先を
右に向けて持って
打つ。

四本目

刀を左手に持ち、
切先を前方に向け
て下げながら打つ。

Chishin School Technique 4

Throw while holding your Katana downward in your left hand with the point forward.	This is a different way to do Technique 4. The Tsuka-gashira, or pommel, is facing to your left and the Kisaki, tip of the sword is facing to your right as you throw.

打ち終ったら、す
ばやく刀を抜いて
構え、

五本目
刀を抜かず、柄を
斜前方に構えて打
つ。

Chishin School Technique 5

Do not draw your sword but push the Tsuka, or handle, diagonally downward. Throw from this position.	After you throw your Shuriken rapidly draw your sword and stand as shown in the illustration.

次に切先を前方に
向け突き出して後、

納刀して終る。

Chishin School Technique 5	
Next, stab forward with the tip of your sword, then…	…sheathe your sword and the technique is over.

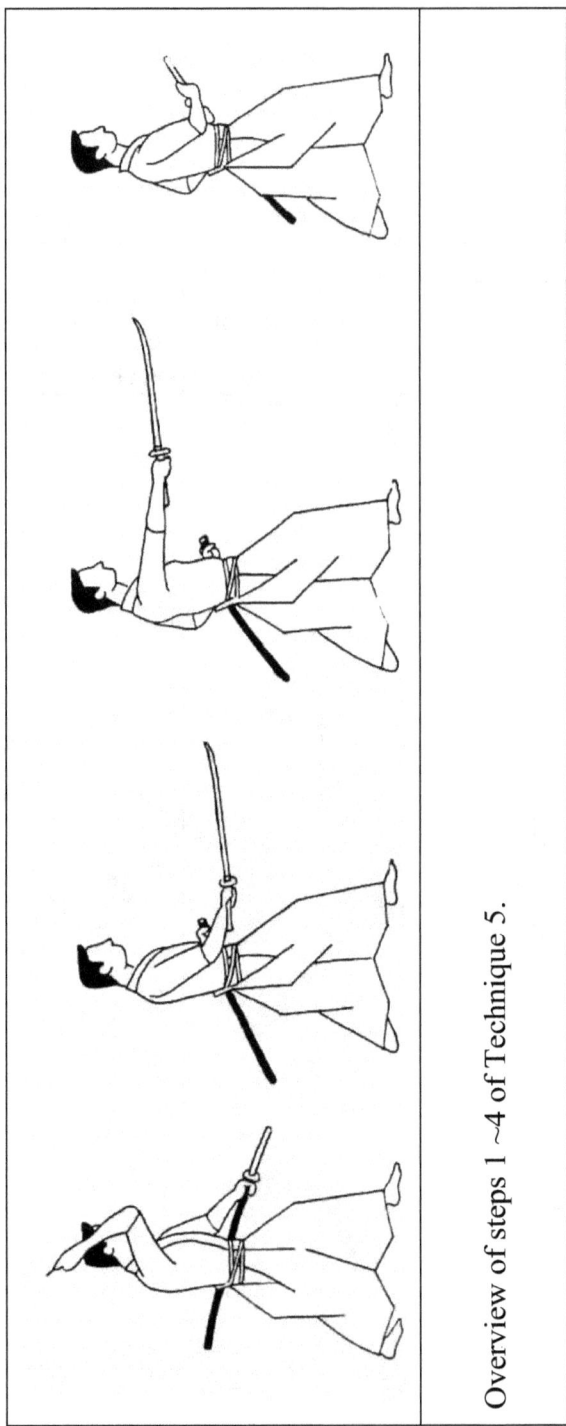

Overview of steps 1 ~4 of Technique 5.

Translator's Note:
The *Tokugawa Museum* has a set of four Chishin School Shuriken in its collection. While unfortunately it is not a set of five, which would directly correlate to this document there is the interesting fact that the Shuriken are of different sizes ranging from the largest at 17.4 centimeters and weighing 160 grams to the smallest being 12.7 cm weighing 72 grams. They are signed by Hoki no kami Fujiwara Nobutaka a hereditary name of a sword-smith school active from the 17th century to the Meiji restoration in 1868.

Yagyu Shin Kage School
&
Shuriken

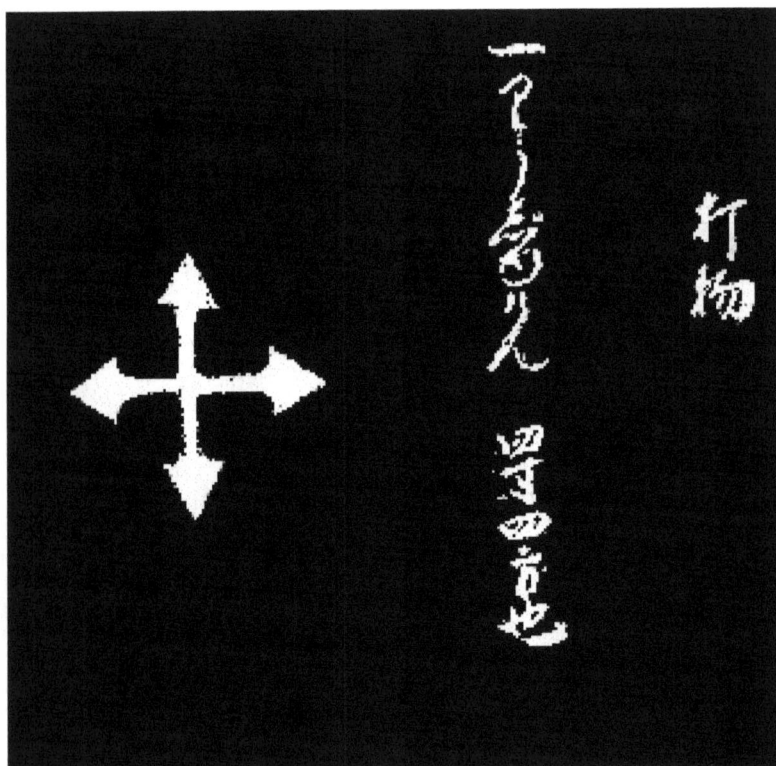

Yagyu and Shuriken

Translator's Introduction:

Unfortunately, Naruse Kanji does not specify in which book he found the description of the duel between Miyamoto Musashi and the Yagyu clan. However, after looking over numerous documents by the Yagu School, I found the word "Shuriken" appears frequently.

Yagyu Sekishusai used the words Shuriken and Juji Shuriken, in a certificate of transmission to Miyoshi Saemon-no-Jo in 1581. These were written:

Shuriken 手裏見 (Hand + Reverse + Observe)

Juji Shuriken 十字手裏見 (Cross + Hand + Reverse + Observe.)

Later, in the *Heiho Kadensho*, Yagyu Munenori, uses the word *Shuji Shuriken* 手字種利劍 (Hand + Kanji + Variety + Use + Sword.) Yagyu Jube, Sekishusai's grandson, uses the same word and Kanji in the *Moon Scroll* 月の抄 which he wrote in 1642.

Most of the references to "Shuriken" do not refer to a projectile weapon, rather they explain how to evaluate your opponent's strategy. However, some of the documents explain how to defend against swords thrown as Shuriken, as Naruse Kanji mentions. The final document discusses carrying Shuriken and also gives specific dimensions.

The first translation in this section is of the Shinkage School Document Naruse Kanji introduced in his discussion of Miyamoto Musashi. He says,

In a Shinkage School document dating from the 15th year of Keicho, there is an illustration of a two-sword technique.

This is referring to an illustrated document Yagyu Sekishusai commissioned in 1601. It was an illustrated scroll of Yagyu Shin Kage School techniques called *Certification in Yagyu School Techniques* which he gave to his friend, a Noh actor. Over a hundred years later, in 1707, descriptions of the techniques were written on the picture by a Yagyu Shinkage school master, Matsudaira Nobusada.

The following page will translate the technique mentioned by Naruse Kanji in his book.

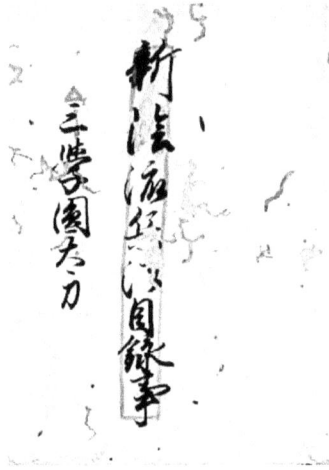

Translation of:
Yagyu Shinkage Ryu
Yagyu New School of the Shadow Sword
　↳ *Certification in Yagyu School Techniques*
　　↳ *The Tengu Scroll*
　　　↳ **Karanbo : Raging Fire Tengu**

This is the illustration Naruse Kanji included, titled Karanbo, Raging Fire Monk.

Below is the illustration from the original *Certification in Yagyu School Techniques,* drawn in 1601 and augmented with text in 1707.

Karanbo : Raging Fire Tengu
Subete Koran Uchimono-dome :
Completely Subduing the Raging Tiger

The attacker (the human) is in a stance with his long sword in his left hand and his short sword in his right hand. When the attacker edges smoothly forward and attacks, raise your sword (you are the Tengu) so your hands act like a shield. The attacker will immediately move smoothly forward with his long sword, so ensure your body has moved well away. There is a Kuden oral transmission.

You should be immovable in face of the attacker's initial gambit, and maintain readiness to cut the Shuriken down. Then look for where you will strike. With regards to cutting down the Shuriken, devote yourself entirely to meeting it with your sword.

There are many Kuden oral transmissions about this.[10]

---

[10] Naruse Kanji interpreted *Karanbo* to refer to the human figure while, in my opinion, based on the text, Karanbo refers to the Tengu. The final Kanji 房 Bo, can mean a Buddhist priest, however some Tengu were originally priests who attained supernatural power. There are also differences in the hand positioning, meaning Naruse Kanji may have seen a different version of this scroll, with a slightly different interpretation.

Translation of:
Heiho Kadensho
↳ Chapter Titled: ***Though there are hundreds of stances you can take, there is only one way to win in the end.***

In 1631 Yagyu Munenori, Muneyoshi's son, wrote about Shuriken in the *Heiho Kadensho* in a chapter titled *Though there are hundreds of stances you can take, there is only one way to win in the end.*

Though there are hundreds of stances you can take, there is only one way to win in the end. What I am referring to by the above words is Shuji Shuriken 手字種利劍. *This means seeing through the deception the enemy is planning, in other words "reading his hands." Employing this way of observing your enemy will allow you to achieve victory. No matter how many sword techniques you train, how many body positions or ways of holding your sword you learn, the only way to win is to focus on Shuji Shuriken.*

The enemy may know many stances and you may know many stances. However this lesson teaches that Shuji Shuriken is the ultimate path to victory. Since this is a Hiden, secret technique, the real Kanji will not be used. Instead Kanji with the same sound but different meanings are employed, thus it is written 手字種利劍 *(Hand + Character + Variety + Use + Sword.)*[11]

---

[11] Clearly in the *Heiho Kadensho* the meaning of Shuriken is about discerning the enemy's intent. However, in a later book *Lessons on Becoming a Polished Jewel* the Shuriken as a weapon is specifically mentioned.

Shuriken in *Lessons on Becoming a Polished Jewel*

Yagyu Munenori wrote *Lessons on Becoming a Polished Jewel* in the 3rd year of Shoho 1645. He gave this book to Nabeshima Hida no Kamai Naoyoshi. It contains various chapters on the sword arts and developing yourself into a better person.

The passage translated on the following page deals with Shuriken. The passage, titled *Uchi Mono*, or *Striking Weapons*, frequently alters between two ways of writing the word Shuriken. One is 手利剣 (Hand + Usage + Sword) and the other is 手裏剣 (Hand + Reverse + Sword.) I have included the Kanji to indicate this switch since I am not sure if this is intentional or the writer simply changing back and forth.

Translation of:

柳生新影流 *Yagyu Shin Kage Ryu*

玉成集 *Lessons on Becoming A Polished Jewel (A Great Human)*

↳打物 *Uchi Mono*   Striking Weapons

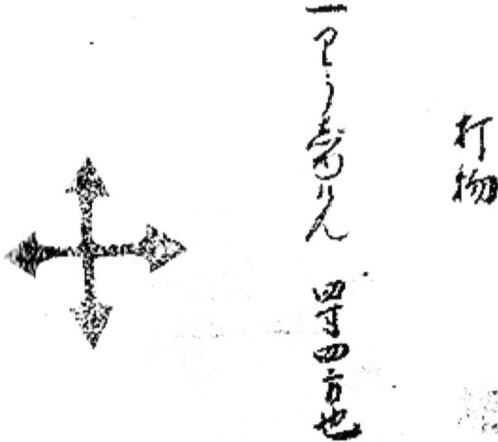

First page of *Uchi Mono*

This is about throwing a Wakizashi, Shoto or whatever you have on you at the time. You can practice with various weapons turning training . However the weapons often fail to hit their mark, and therefore should not be relied upon. You should hold your spirit in a state of readiness with both your inward intended attack and outward feint ready. However at any point the outer can become the inner and vice versa. This duality of outward and inward changing freely is called Hyo-Ri. In combat, you should be able to employ either but not be beholden to either. This is essential if you are to glean the enemy's intention.

If is the hand that releases the Shuriken 手利剣. The way you strike with a spear, halberd or sword depends on the situation. However, at the same time, you cannot be completely reliant on your weapon, and maintain readiness (to strike).

This same thinking applies when you unexpectedly encounter opponents armed with rifles or bows. Thus you should always carry one on your person.

Despite the fact that Uchi Mono, projectile weapons, like bows and rifles are far more accurate, I still recommend always carrying Shuriken. Carry Shuriken but do not rely on them exclusively. Keeping Shuriken on your person is an important lesson for warriors. There are many kinds of weapons you can throw, and, in fact, you can throw anything. These are just two examples.
An old document sayeth:

If your enemy throws a Shuriken 手利剣 at you, he is expecting that strike to grant him victory. Therefore, if it strikes your technique, abandon your technique and win the duel.

If it strikes your face then abandon your face and win the duel.

If it strikes your fighting spirit, then abandon your fighting spirit and win the duel.

If it strikes your body, then abandon your body and win the duel. With that small sacrifice you can achieve victory.

There are a great many secret teachings regarding this.

When speaking of Shuriken 手利剣, there are a great many ways to throw. There is a teaching about Nakatabi, In the Middle (of Combat,) Shuriken 手裏剣. There are many kinds of Shuriken 手裏剣 used to draw the enemy's attention your way. There are many secret techniques regarding this.

Further, there are many Kuden, oral transmissions, regarding how to respond when your enemy throws a Shuriken 手利剣 at you. The first thing you should do when the opponent is readying his strike is to identify the place he seeks to achieve victory. Once you understand this use The Three Ways of Victory.

There are many secret teachings regarding this.

右鼻紙に入て持ても打つなり

Carry these wrapped in paper handkerchief. They can be thrown while still wrapped

Uchi mono
Striking
Things

打物

りゅうしゅ剣

Sanko
Three
Lights

三光

Ryushu Ken
Ryushu
Sword

Each arm is
4 Sun, 12
cm long

四寸四方也

Each arm is
4 Sun, 12
cm long

四寸四方也

Miyamoto Musashi and Shuriken
End

www.ingramcontent.com/pod-product-compliance
Lightning Source LLC
Chambersburg PA
CBHW070920270326
41927CB00011B/2652